No Man's Land is an informative, well-researched, and artfully crafted work by a master in his field, arguably St. Lucia's most prominent writer. Digs deep into the meat of his country's political system to extrapolate the root causes of a system with built-in mechanisms for graft, kickbacks, nepotism, corruption, and less than covert thieving by politicians, while the governed are clueless or powerless or complicitly tolerant. A pointed and timely work highly recommended for political front liners, academics, students, and all interested in understanding and willing to help shape and re-shape the Caribbean and its attendant institutions.

—**Modeste Downes, author of** *A Lesson on Wings,* *Theatre of the Mind,* **and** *Phases*

NO MAN'S LAND

A Political Introspection of St. Lucia

Also by Anderson Reynolds

My Father Is No Longer There (memoir, 2019)

The Stall Keeper (novel, 2017)

The Struggle for Survival: An historical, political, and socioeconomic perspective of St. Lucia (creative non-fiction, 2003)

Death by Fire (novel, 2001)

NO MAN'S LAND

A Political Introspection of St. Lucia

Anderson Reynolds

JAKO BOOKS

Vieux Fort, New York, London

Published in the United States by Jako Books, a division of Jako Productions.

First Jako Books Edition, January 2021

www.jakoproductions.com

Library of Congress Control Number (LCCN): 2020951031

ISBN-13:
978-1-7332913-2-3

For my hometown, Vieux Fort, my continued source of inspiration and dedication; may you fulfill your great promise.

Sir George Frederick Lawrence Charles
(7 June 1916 – 26 June 2004)

First adult suffrage head of government (chief minister).
Credited with politically enfranchising St. Lucians.

CONTENTS

Special thanks to Modeste Downes, Peter Lansiquot, Dr. Prosper Raynold, Julius James, Dr. James Fletcher, Wentworth Reynolds, and Alexander Clarke for their comments and suggestions from which *No Man's Land* has profited greatly.

Sir John George Melvin Compton, KCMG, PC
(29 April 1925 – 7 September 2007)

St. Lucia's first and only premier and first and longest
serving prime minister. Regarded by many as the Father of
the Nation and St. Lucia's Man of the Century. Credited
with building the country's physical and economic infrastructure.

Part I

The Chastanet Ultimatum

George William Odlum
(24 June 1934 – 28 September 2003)

Minister of government. Regarded as one of St. Lucia's greatest orators. Credited with raising the nation's socio-political consciousness to unprecedented heights.

1

BY HOOK OR BY CROOK

As the 17th general elections (18th if one includes two elections in 1987 as opposed to one) of the universal suffrage era draws near, many St. Lucians, especially St. Lucia Labour Party (SLP) supporters, are convinced that the prime minister, Allen Chastanet, is ruining the country and has proven unfit to rule.[1,2]

However, it is troubling that SLP operatives seem to be using the notion that Allen Chastanet is destroying the country as an ultimatum—*Vote Labour or suffer the Allen Chastanet train wreck*—and believe that a United Workers Party (UWP or Flambeau) defeat at the polls is a forgone conclusion; meaning, lambasting the prime minister and highlighting his perceived misdeeds are the totality of what some SLP politicians may think they have to do to win the general elections. If so, will they not be guilty of underestimating Chastanet's UWP and setting themselves up to suffer a repeat of their 2016 election defeat?

It is also troubling that SLP is giving the impression that the biggest problem facing St. Lucia is Allen Chastanet, and getting rid of him will return the country to happy days. Equipped with the Chastanet Ultimatum, SLP may erroneously believe it does not have to undergo the soul-searching required to ascertain what went wrong in 2016 (and thus avoid repeating history) when it allowed a disintegrating UWP to take over the reins of government, a party that has not found its footing since the mythical John Compton, considered the Father of the Nation, gave up the party leadership (in 1997). Indeed, the only time SLP has defeated a Compton-led UWP was in 1979 when the SLP ticket presented an unprecedented number of college-educated candidates, not least among them the great George Odlum, a candidate for St. Lucia's Man of the Century, credited with raising the political and social consciousness of the nation to un-precedented heights,[3] a topic revisited in the forthcoming book, *They Called Him Brother George: Portrait of a Caribbean Politician,*[4] by Reynolds and Lansiquot.

The 2016 UWP that defeated the incumbent SLP was in such chaos that up to a few weeks before elections it was doubtful that Stephenson King and Peter Lenard Montoute, two key politi-cians and long-serving stalwarts of the UWP, would join the race.

SLP soul-searching is critical because, besides enabling a crumbling and thus ill-prepared UWP to form the 2016 government, in some ways Chastanet is Labour's creation. Notice it was SLP that introduced the citizenship-by-investment program (CIP) (with its accompanying loopholes) that some regard as tantamount to putting the country up for sale. Dr. James Fletcher, a Chevening Global Changemaker, author of *Governing in a Small Caribbean Island State*, and arguably the most stellar and nationally and in-ternationally respected minister of the Kenny Anthony government era, has since expressed misgivings about having supported the CIP.[5] Notice that the Desert Star Holdings (DSH)[6] proposal, which many viewed as gifting the best of Vieux Fort to a foreign entity and which formed the basis of the agreement Chastanet signed, was on the table long before the prime minister came to power.

Notice also that leading to the 2016 general elections the SLP government had left plenty of unfinished business. Even with a head start the government failed to complete St. Jude Hospital in four years, and it could have had several additional months to work on the hospital had it not called early elections. The assignment of the contract for the Hewanorra International Airport PPP (public-private partnership) project was left hanging, allowing Chastanet to abandon the concept. The construction of the Vieux Fort Administrative Complex was started only a few months before the 2016 elections, making it possible for Chastanet to easily abort the project, which he did. It would appear that SLP left a vacuum that Chastanet was happy to fill, which, according to many, particularly SLP supporters, has produced disastrous results.

As an example of one such disastrous result, consider the DSH horse racetrack, which was supposed to be a Teo Ah Khing project. However, after millions of the country's dollars have been poured into the project, after the Vieux Fort landscape has been damaged and compromised, and after it has become clear, and as both Allen Chastanet and Invest St. Lucia intimated, this is a financially infeasible and unprofitable enterprise,[7,8,9] or at best a loss leader, one suspects that Teo Ah Khing has pulled out of the project. Nonetheless, one also suspects that to avoid losing face, Chastanet has had no choice but to continue unilaterally with it, leaving many to ask: *since when is government in the business of horse racing?*

The Chastanet Ultimatum also means that, other than to get rid of Chastanet, some SLP politicians may think they do not have to justify why St. Lucians, who soundly rejected them in 2016, should elect them in the 2021 elections. Nor do they have to tell St. Lucians what they will do differently this time around to merit their vote. Nor how they will better position St. Lucia in this post-COVID-19, rapid technologically changing world. They seem displeased with DSH and outraged over Chastanet's approach to CIP, but they have not told the nation (and may not see a need to) how they plan to modify these programs/projects or whether they plan to scrap them altogether. They have not told the nation (and may not see a need to) what they are going to do for its communities; for each electoral district, what are the five to ten areas of priority they will focus on. It seems that this time around SLP's manifesto may simply have Chastanet conducting a runaway train, or holding a gun to the head of the citizenry, with the byline: *Don't worry about what SLP will do for you, worry about what Chastanet will do to you.*

Do Not Let The Politicians Off The Hook

In this political cycle, the SLP campaign slogan seems to be: Chastanet-must-go. However, the question each voter ought to ask of their would be SLP district rep and the would be SLP government is: what are you going to do for my district? Meaning, other than replacing the Allen Chastanet administration, other than the Chastanet Ultimatum, what plans do you have for my district and the country? In fact, each district should go further and present a list of what they would like to see take place in their district, and to find out what steps a SLP government would take to implement them.

For example, following is the response of a thirty-year-old, born and raised Vieux Fortian, when he was asked over the phone that as the prime minister and the district rep of Vieux Fort, what more could Kenny Anthony have done for Vieux Fort.

> Kenny could have: (1) build a proper bus terminal, (2) establish a cruise ship berth, (3) organize a proper food market, (4) establish better sporting facilities and a sport academy, (5) modernize the

Vieux Fort library, (6) bring certain government facilities to the South, like passport office, etc., (7) bring in more manufacturing industries, (8) upgrade and revitalize Port Vieux Fort, (9) place greater focus on agriculture, (10) develop the waterfront as an attraction, and the list goes on.

Bear in mind this is just one person's off-the-cuff list. Clearly, each district can be expected to have definite ideas of what they would like to see happen in their community. So, although many may agree that Chastanet is unfit to rule and UWP has to go, they would be well advised to not let SLP off the hook, to not let SLP use the Chastanet Ultimatum to compel them, threaten them, intimidate them to vote SLP back in power. As a prerequisite for their vote, communities across the island must insist on what SLP will do for them.

Likewise, Vieux Fort's Friends of Labour and the great defender of Vieux Fort, the Vieux Fort Concerned Citizens Coalition For Change (VFCCCC), should be reminded that now is the most advantageous time to present their development plan for Vieux Fort to the would be SLP administration and the would be SLP Vieux Fort South district rep. Now is the time to harvest their decades of steadfast loyalty to the Labour Party, which their district rep calls defiance. Now is the time to hold their support as an ultimatum to insist that SLP address the development needs of Vieux Fort as per their proposed development plan.

For once, defy the history of Vieux Fort always being dictated to by outsiders, and grab the initiative. VFCCCC members have been resolute, and rightly so, in their opposition to the terms and conditions of the DSH agreement, which many view as atrocious to the interest of Vieux Fort and St. Lucia, but what guarantee do they have that a Labour administration will discontinue Chastanet's Dubai Palm Island and Miami Beach dreams? This time around, Vieux Fort must stop being subservient to the system and insist that the system work for Vieux Fort.

Supporting and voting for a political party no matter what (which Dr. Kenny Anthony calls defiance), even defending its misdeeds or remaining silent in the face of its atrocities, is detrimental to the country, is tantamount to rewarding bad behavior; and, as every parent knows, the worst thing one can do in raising children is to reward their bad behavior. It is this that may have emboldened Allen Chastanet and given him cover to, according to SLP supporters, run roughshod over the country. And it is this that enables district reps to smugly ignore or neglect the concerns and development imperatives of their constituencies, knowing full well their votes are secure.

Therefore, do not be like the avid Labour supporter (a retired primary school teacher and labor union leader) who said that he does not care about the issues, all he cares about is to give Chastanet enough rope to hang himself so that SLP can get back in power. What good is such a mentality to one's community, to one's country?

Voters should also call upon the media and all 17 of St. Lucia's electoral districts to insist on nationally televised and social media plug-in debates between the district rep candidates of each district, and a debate between the leaders of the contesting political parties. This way, side by side, voters can compare what the candidates plan to offer their districts and the country. It is time St. Lucia moves beyond the noise, bluster, and hype of political public meetings and zero in on the crux of the matter — what exactly have the politicians in store for the country?

There is no shortage of development ideas or plans for Vieux Fort[10] and St. Lucia,[11] but there is a *shortage of political will and desire*. Of course, the politicians will complain that as a small, poor country their hands are tied; there is much they want to do, but so few means to do it with. But this is misleading. St. Lucia may be a poor country (actually it is classified as an upper-middle income country), but within one or two terms in office some of its elected politicians have metamorphosed from hand-to-mouth existence to millionaires. And the idea is not to sit down and wait for the government to do for one's community but to partner with one's district rep and together find the answers and the solutions.

Once upon a time most St. Lucians probably thought the country was too poor to establish enough schools for all the nation's children to attend secondary school. Yet, no sooner had Dr. Kenny Anthony and his Labour Party come to power (in 1997) after a 33 year drought (interrupted by 3 years of an ill-fated SLP rule), miraculously the country had enough schools for every child to attend secondary school; so much so that today there is an overcapacity of secondary schools. Now, looking back, one is almost tempted to say that the populace was deliberately kept uneducated to serve the interest of the politicians. Think of the lost opportunity of generation upon generation of the nation's children denied a secondary education. What does this say? It says *often the development or progress of the country is not a matter of resources or know-how but a matter of will and desire*. If the politicians were as keen to develop the country as they are keen to win votes and engage in economic extraction then the country would be on a much higher plane.

Just as the once-upon-a-time shortage of secondary schools was not a matter of poverty, *St. Lucia's economic stagnation isn't a matter of limited resources nor a matter of a lack of knowhow*. As Peter Prescod[12,13,14] lucidly points out, "clear prescriptions" for the ills of the economy were articulated by Dr. Reginald Darius, former permanent secretary in the ministry of finance, which have since been echoed by the Caribbean Development Bank (CDB), the IMF, and Dr. Kenny Anthony in his May 24, 2013 budget address. None of the prescriptions have been implemented, *not because of a lack of resources or knowhow but because of a lack of will and/or desire.*

Now, forgetting they were in power for three of the past five terms and for two of these terms they had an overwhelming majority, SLP politicians and supporters may tell voters: *Don't worry, we will deal with all this afterwards, let's not fight among ourselves, the priority now is to get rid of the Allen Chastanet "monster". We must stop the Allen Chastanet train wreck at all costs.*

But by now voters should know too well what happens when they allow politicians to use them as their tool. They help perpetuate a vicious cycle. Election time the politicians come begging for votes as if it is a matter of life and death. They come like Jesus Christ, so humble, so sincere, so generous, so they-have-seen-the-errors-of-their-ways, only to discard the people and treat them with disdain as soon as they get in power, engage in economic extraction at the expense of the masses, and then after five years come begging yet again for votes.

VFCCCC and other community groups, it is, as now, when the politicians come begging for your votes, regardless of the Chastanet Ultimatum, that you can exert the greatest influence. Unless the politicians can commit to a definite plan of action for your community and country, refuse to support them, refuse to attend their rallies, refuse to get on their platforms. Hold them up to your plan of action throughout their term in office. When they do not uphold their end of the bargain, shame them. March against them if that is what it takes. Placard them if that is all that can be done. Hold them accountable.

2

THE CRUX OF THE MATTER

The Biggest Problem Facing St. Lucia

Allen Chastanet may have mishandled the country (a claim that will be evaluated in Part III), but he is not the biggest problem the country faces, neither is COVID-19. On the contrary, the prime minister may have done the country a favor because if, according to some, he has taken things to their ultimate conclusion, to where no other politician has taken them, he has highlighted the defects of the country's system of governance, which is the greatest threat to its democracy, its social, political, and economic development. If Chastanet has run down the country unchecked, that is because he operates within a political and governance structure, which was none of his making, that enables such outcomes. What separates Chastanet from his predecessors might be more a matter of style than a matter of substance. He may have been bolder and more blatant in his disregard of the citizenry and the nation's laws and institutions, but he is just a product of the system. He may have taken things to the extreme, but he is not alone in abusing the system.

Such misadventures as Rochamel[1], Grynberg[2], and Le Paradis[3] (an environmental disaster that receives little attention) cannot be attributed to him. Yet this is only what one knows about, what may be just the tip of the iceberg. If the Desert Star Holdings (DSH) agreements[4] had not been leaked, all what one would have known and seen about DSH would have been eye-popping development plans/designs,[5,6] and who does not like development? So, the question is, how much has the country sacrificed and how much money have politicians pocketed for some of the development projects that have taken place and of which St. Lucians are proud?

Unless pertinent documents are leaked, one will never know for sure of government exploitation of the country.

Chastanet is not totally to blame for DSH and for the CIP; Kenny Anthony's administration laid the groundwork for these. Chastanet may have just driven things to their lowest common denominator. The political and governance factory can manufacture anything but such undesirable products, such atrocious outcomes. One can throw away, destroy each defective batch of products, but as if by design the factory will keep churning them out.

The system Chastanet inherited and the system that gave birth to him is one with no campaign finance reform. It is a system that enables government ministers to accept cash from foreign governments for diplomatic relations. It is a system that enables ministers to insist on bribes to allow foreign entities to establish businesses. A system that enables ministers to establish shell companies to direct patronage to their pockets, or to trade the awarding of government contracts for campaign financing or other forms of kickbacks. A system of seemingly no recourse when government violates the laws of the land and corrupts or undermines its statutory institutions.

A system where prime ministers can unilaterally, without even the consent of their Cabinet, sign agreements putting the country into multi-million-dollar holes. A system where there are few checks and balances in government; where the district reps form both the legislature (House of Assembly) and the executive (Cabinet); where there is little accountability to the voters; where policies and projects are implemented with little voter participation, consultation, much less consensus; and where the only time voters have a say is every five years at the voting booth.

In economics and industrial organization there is a structure-conduct-performance paradigm in which the structure of an industry (number and size of firms, ease of entry, availability of substitute goods or services, regulation, etc.) influences the behavior or conduct of firms (investment, monopolistic behavior, collusion, advertising, price fixing), which affects their performance (economic efficiency, profitability, wealth accumulation). The same applies to political systems and to any system one can think of. The structure of the political system (the composition of Cabinet and Parliament, the rules that govern their functioning) determines the behavior of elected politicians (dictatorship, economic extraction, lack of transparency and accountability, trampling the rights of citizens). And the behavior of government and elected politicians affects national performance (economic growth, poverty, wealth distribution, health, social and economic wellbeing, quality of life, etc.). In search of all these nice and desirable outcomes, voters keep alternating between SLP and UWP as if they are the problem; they are the disease and not just the symptoms of the disease.

At this political juncture, SLP would like St. Lucians to believe that Chastanet is the cancer, the problem, and as soon as they get rid of Chastanet it will be happy days again. The rest of the story is well known. When voters change UWP and put in SLP, they then realize that the cancer may have retreated a little, but it is still there. It did not go away. So next election, like a yoyo, they return to UWP. Instead of redesigning the factory, they keep wasting their time discarding defective batches of products, expecting the next batch of products to meet their expectations, un-mindful of the fact that as if by design the factory can produce anything but defective products.

When Sub-Saharan African countries like Sierra Leone, Ghana, Kenya and Zambia gained their independence, there was gleeful anticipation of the social, political, and economic advance-ment that would follow. They thought all they had to do was kick out the evil colonial powers, such that their leaders who made it all come to pass became overnight heroes, knights in shining armor. Like the epic tales, they had faced great dangers and over-come formidable obstacles and foes to bring home the elixir that would heal the nation and make the country overflow with milk and honey.

Sadly, what many were not fully cognizant of was that the colonial powers had established extractive political and economic institutions in these countries, which, according to Acemoglu and Robinson[7], in their book *Why Nations Fail: The Origins of Power, Prosperity, and Poverty*, is a recipe for impoverishment. Extractive political institutions obtain when power is absolutist, i.e., the dis-tribution of power is narrow and unconstrained, and/or when there is a lack of political centralization or state centralization. Ex-tractive economic institutions are designed to extract income and wealth from one subset of society (usually the majority) to benefit a different subset (usually a minority political elite).

The West Indies slave plantation system was an extreme ex-ample of an extractive political and economic system. The white minority enjoyed absolutist political power with few constraints over the black population, and the slave plantation economy was designed to extract all surplus production beyond subsistence for the benefit of the minority white population.

So with an inheritance of extractive institutions, rather than realizing post-independence progress and prosperity, these Sub-Saharan African countries plunged into greater social and eco-nomic despair, some of them even becoming failed states, their home-grown leaders, once overnight heroes, proving to be even more evil and oppressive than the colonial rulers they replaced. The lesson is clear. Changing the players while leaving the structure and rules intact can be tantamount to digging a deeper grave. The only way to realize the performance, the outcome, voters desire is to change the structure of the political and governing institutions which would change the behavior of elected politicians and hence the performance, the progress of the country.

So how does one restructure the system to realize the promised land? Well, just as there is no shortage of development ideas and plans, there is no shortage of ideas[8,9] on how to change the constitution, the structure of governance, and the political process to ensure better and greater representation, accountability, and voter participation, and to prevent the excesses of which the Chastanet administration has been accused. Chapter 16 will cover in greater detail the subject of constitutional reform and the making of a more inclusive and democratic government.

The constitution of St. Lucia stipulates that any alteration to the constitution must be supported by the votes of at least two-thirds to three-quarters of all members of the House, depending on which section of the constitution is under such consideration. Since statehood (1967), only four administrations have had at least a two-thirds majority in the house, and only three have had at least a three-quarters majority. In all of Sir John's dominance of St. Lucian politics, only once did he muster a two-thirds or greater majority. That was in 1982 when, following the SLP government debacle, UWP won 14 seats, representing 82% of the 17 seats on offer. The two consecutive landslide victories (1997 & 2001) of the Kenny Anthony-led SLP account for the other two times that an administration has enjoyed at least a three-quarters majority.[10]

Constitutional reform can be a lengthy process, so it may take an administration desirous of such change and with the requisite majority in the House of Assembly multiple terms to achieve.

Hence the party and the prime minister who has been best positioned to change the constitution and the structure of governance
is the SLP administration of 1997-2006 with Kenny Anthony at
the helm, holder of a PhD in law from the University of Birming-
ham. Constitutional reform was not attempted during that period. Nonetheless, it turns out that an overwhelming majority in
the house would have been a non-issue because *the accomplish-
ment of most things is more a matter of will and desire than a matter of
resources.* When, in 2015, after several years (2004 -2011) in the
making, the Constitutional Reform Commission presented its report to the House for consideration, it was rejected by a vote of
17-0 (follow Rick Wayne for House of Assembly deliberations on
the matter[11]).

The irony is that it was the House of Assembly in 2004 under
the control of Kenny Anthony's SLP administration that decreed
the Constitutional Reform Commission, yet 11 years later (2015)
not one of the SLP district reps in the once again Labour controlled House of Assembly voted in favor of constitutional reform. Leaving one to wonder whether the Constitutional Reform
Commission was just SLP's way of appeasing the populace with
no intention of following through, in much the same way some
have accused Kenny Anthony of appeasing Vieux Fortians with
handouts, footpaths, and promenades while avoiding the serious
and substantive business of job creation and economic upliftment.

This result suggests that even if SLP were to win all 17 of the
seats on offer in this coming election, unless something drastic
intervenes, like a people's revolution for constitutional reform,
one should expect business as usual. So the notion that, with the
expulsion of Chastanet, the country will return to happy days, so
for now everyone must focus strictly on getting rid of "this nemesis" called Allen Chastanet, and all other things shall be added
unto the country, is a delusion within a delusion.

The politicians' (on both sides of the isle) demonstrated take
on constitutional reform should surprise no one, for most political

scientists will agree that the primary objective of a politician is to get elected and to stay in power, and it is a rare feat when someone gives up power willingly. Looking after the best interest of their constituency and that of the country is of secondary or incidental concern to politicians.

The 2020 US presidential election presents a perfect example of the overriding imperative of politicians. Outstanding Republican lawmakers, paragons of democracy, refused to recognize Joe Biden as the president-elect, willing to sacrifice all what they hold dear about America, not because they are convinced of the fraudulence of the poll results, but because they don't want to risk the wrath of Donald Trump, who remains popular with Republican voters, and thus suffer political reprisals.

This means that the only way citizens can ensure that the interest of politicians are aligned with theirs is through diligent and unceasing monitoring and advocacy, and through protest action. In other words, making sure that politicians pay a heavy price for deviating from the interest of their charge. By extension, the only way constitutional reform will take place is by people power, by a revolution. So Richard Frederick's attempted island-wide motorcade[12] (which led to the arrest of SLP activist, Christopher Hunte, for what the authorities called "unlawful" anti-government motorcade) to protest against the UWP government and to help oust Chastanet from power, not unlike how Chastanet and his UWP had expelled him from the party,[13] is misplaced effort; the country would have been better served if he had led a motorcade, or better yet a people's revolution, for constitutional reform.

The above admonishment is not just for the benefit of the populace. The election of SLP may depend on it, the realization of the Chastanet-must-go slogan may hinge on it. Because it is not clear that the tired Labour mantra of playing victim, of rescuing the poor and down-trodden, of what the big, bad wolf of a Compton or a Chastanet is doing to the country, of fear mongering akin to the Christian hell fire and brimstone threat to win souls (votes), will cut it. Based on anecdotal information, one suspects that business people think Flambeau as opposed to Labour is better for business. Moreover, if Chastanet is trampling the nation's laws and institutions, then he is creating an environment in which businesses feel freer to wheel and deal, to disregard or bend restraining laws and standards. So the Chastanet slogan may not resonate as strongly with them.

Also, it is doubtful that the youth, who may care more about jobs, scholarships, and telecommunication gadgets, than about corruption (which they attribute to both parties), will be inspired by the slogan Chastanet-must-go. Yes, the slogan is likely to motivate the SLP base to campaign and join the voting queue. But it is also likely to sharpen the battle swords of the entrenched Flambeaus. So then the question: Is the Chastanet Ultimatum, the Chastanet train wreck, menacing enough and is the Chastanet-must-go slogan powerful enough to bring out the undecided voters, those sitting on the fence unimpressed with Chastanet but to whom the reasons they voted out Labour in 2016 remain?

Beware of Underestimating Allen Chastanet

It seems that in the Kenny Anthony era, SLP has kept making the mistake of underestimating the UWP. They were stunned in 2006 when a geriatric, though larger-than-life persona, John Compton, led his embattled UWP to victory. During that election campaign, so confident was the Labour Party, having racked two consecutive landslide victories, that they took to ridiculing John Compton's advanced age, calling him a "toothless tiger."[14]

SLP suffered an even greater shock when in 2016 it was soundly defeated by a falling-apart UWP, led, not by the mythical and heroic Sir John Compton, but by Allen Chastanet, a political novice.

In the 2016 election, UWP won 11 seats to SLP's 6, they garnered 46,165 votes or 54.76% of all valid votes compared to SLP's 37,172 or 44.09% of valid votes.[10] Yet SLP was lucky to win those 6 seats, several of which were won by narrow margins. Dr. Kenny Anthony won by 240 votes, his narrowest margin of victory (the next closest was by 624 votes in 2006) since representing Vieux Fort. If Dr. Keith Mondesir, the opposition UWP candidate, had put up a credible campaign, the results of the 2016 elections may have stunned Kenny Anthony and the Labour Party even more strongly.

It would appear that not only has SLP formed a habit of underestimating the UWP, it has formed a habit of losing to seemingly weak UWP oppositions.

Now, in 2021, the nation is at another juncture of its political history. Allen Chastanet is being vilified as an enemy of the state. Many have opined he has proven unfit to rule. Some have even said that at the end of a Chastanet second term there will be nothing left in the country worth saving. It would appear that, like in 2006 and again in 2016, Chastanet's UWP is teetering and destined to fail in its electoral bid. So SLP may well be thinking that all what it will take to topple what some regard as a beleaguered and discredited UWP government is an ever so gentle breeze of the mantra Chastanet-must-go.

Woe be unto those who ignore history. There is a good chance that the Chastanet-must-go mantra, and the Chastanet Ultimatum are likely to fail. Notice that, however awful was President Donald Trump, he gave the world quite a scare; the 2020 US presidential election results were closer than many would have predicted. Many Americans were and remain unimpressed with and uninspired by President-elect Joe Biden. So chances are if not for Trump's callous and bizarre approach to COVID-19, Biden's campaign ploy of simply presenting himself as the decent and sane guy would have failed. SLP has no such luck. To the great relief of many St. Lucians, Allen Chastanet handled the COVID-19 threat admirably; he followed the advice of the health professionals. So unlike Joe Biden, COVID-19 cannot come to the rescue of SLP. Therefore, SLP's only sure savior is inspiring leadership.

SLP needs a new message, a new narrative, a new direction, a message of hope, a message of engaging, accountable, transparent and participatory government, a message of constitutional reform, a message of not taking the populace for granted, a message in tune with the 21st century, a message of closing the gap between St. Lucia and first world countries, a message or vision of moral, social and economic upliftment backed up by a concrete plan. A message of rescuing the country from its persistently high unemployment. A message to inspire all St. Lucians, young and old alike, SLP and UWP supporters alike, businesses and households alike. SLP needs to discard the Chastanet Ultimatum, stop using it as a crutch, as a smokescreen to avoid getting down to the serious business of engineering a new path for the upliftment of the country.

Andrew Antoine, a cultural and social activist who claims to have known Philip J. Pierre for over 30 years, said[15] that the SLP political leader is:

> A humble, honest, caring, principled, and very intelligent man… his persona, his demonstrated firm grasp of local, regional and international issues, and empathy with our people, will guide us through the difficult times of rebuilding St. Lucia after this disastrous Allen Chastanet-led UWP administration is voted from office.

And Peter Lansiquot, an economist, former St. Lucian diplomat, and a self-professed SLP stalwart, who like Andrew Antoine has known Philip J. Pierre for over three decades, is not only convinced of the leadership and professional acumen of the SLP political leader but asserts that he has more than earned the right to lead his party.[15]

Phillip J. Pierre is much better prepared as an Opposition Leader than has been the case of any other leader of the Opposition of any political party in Saint Lucia's history. History also shows that apart from Julian R. Hunte, Philip J. Pierre is the first Labour leader in over four decades, who has had to fully earn his spurs through long and dedicated work in his Constituency and in the Party. Hon Pierre has to date received no favors or golden handshakes from anyone, and has earned his place at the maximum leadership of the Party...Hon Philip J. Pierre, apart from former Prime Minister, Hon John Compton, is the first Opposition Leader in the history of Saint Lucia, without having been a Prime Minister, to hold professional qualifications and extensive practical experience in the field of Economics, Economic Development, Accounting and Finance.

If, as Andrew Antoine and Peter Lansiquot intimated, Philip J. Pierre as prime minister has both the leadership and technocratic attributes to usher in a new and improved era in the nation's life, then one can think of no better way to signal and realize this change and to improve his chances of winning the elections and sitting on the throne than to embrace constitutional reform (thus more inclusive political and economic institutions) and to make it part of his election platform and to impress upon the nation that to implement constitutional reform he would need at least 14 electoral seats. If all this were to manifest, it will set Philip J. Pierre apart from all politicians who came before him, and history may record him as the hero who captured and brought home the elixir that set the country on a fresh path of unprecedented holistic development. A feat not even John Compton, the Father of the Nation; George Odlum, the great enlightener; Dr. Kenny

D. Anthony, the shepherd who steered the nation into the 21st century, could lay claim to.

This may sound like fiction. But it is not. Earlier it was mentioned that extractive institutions are a recipe for impoverishment. Well, turning once more to Acemoglu and Robinson, the opposite of extractive political and economic institutions is inclusive political and economic institutions. Inclusive economic institutions foster broad based participation in economic activities and allow individuals the freedom to make economic choices. Inclusive political institutions are centralized and are pluralistic in that power is broadly distributed and is subject to constraints or checks and balances. According to the authors, the rich nations of the world are invariably those with a high degree of inclusive political and economic institutions. Therefore, with constitutional reform in St. Lucia fostering more inclusive institutions, one can expect renewed economic progress.

By now, SLP supporters may be wondering why the exclusive focus on SLP to implement constitutional reform? Why is the UWP being absolved of the responsibility? Why are they being let off the hook? The answer is rather straightforward. First, it is SLP that was convincingly defeated in the previous elections and that is now seeking to regain power, therefore they are the ones most in need of an election campaign makeover. And as discussed above, their current election prescription of Chastanet-must-go and the Chastanet Ultimatum is likely to fail.

Second, as opposed to the UWP, previous SLP administrations have demonstrated an interest in constitutional and local government reform. For example, the Kenny Anthony-led Labour Party had established the Constitutional Reform Commission and also a task force on re-instituting and strengthening local government.

Third, SLP has prided itself on being a progressive party, a great champion of the common man, of equality. After all, it was the likes of George Charles, first as a member of the St. Lucia

Workers Union and then as a member of the St. Lucia Labour Party, who spearheaded the St. Lucia labour movement, laid the foundation of workers' rights, and helped usher in universal adult suffrage. It was Labour stalwarts like George Odlum and Peter Josie who were credited with raising the social and political consciousness of St. Lucians to unprecedented heights. And it was Kenny Anthony's SLP government that brought about such fundamental paradigm shifts as universal secondary education, and the creation of a kinder and gentler country. Thus, considering SLP's history of progressiveness, their supporters should not be surprised that their party is being called upon to implement constitutional reform. For what can be more progressive than reforms that give the common man a greater voice in government, afford the masses better and more responsive political representation, and enable governments to work in the best interest of the country?

Fourth, if, as is being suggested, the Chastanet UWP government is running roughshod over the country, disregarding its laws and statutory bodies, the very conduct constitutional reform is designed to preclude, one can hardly expect such a government to implement constitutional reform. And even if they were to make constitutional reform part of their campaign platform, they would likely have a hard time convincing voters of their sincerity.

Therefore, at this time, SLP represents the country's best hope of implementing constitutional reform.

Part II

St. Lucia Elects a
White Prime Minister

Dr. Kenny Davis Anthony
(born 8 January 1951)

Three-term prime minister of St. Lucia. Credited with advancing the country's social infrastructure, shepherding the country into the 21 century, and creating a kinder and gentler country.

3

AN INTRIGUING QUESTION

I n Part I, it was intimated that SLP has much more work to do
to win the 2021 general elections than simply chanting Chastanet-must-go and threatening voters with the Chastanet Ultimatum — *Vote Labour or suffer the Allen Chastanet train wreck*. It
was also pointed out that one thing SLP may need to work on is
to do the soul-searching required to ascertain what went wrong
in 2016 and thus avoid repeating history when a disintegrating
UWP was allowed to take over the reins of government.

So now the narrative goes back to 2016 to throw some light
on how the Chastanet-led UWP was able to capture the crown.

The inquiry begins with an intriguing question.

As the 2016 St. Lucia general election campaign raged on,
and the island's two major political parties paraded, rallied, mo-
torcaded and conducted public political meetings in every nook
and cranny of the island, leaving no stone, or rather no voter un-
turned, probably the question uppermost on the minds of many
St. Lucians was: would St. Lucia elect a white prime minister?

The question reared its head ever since Allen Chastanet, a
white St. Lucian, or an almost white St. Lucian, had maneuvered

to become the political leader of his party, the UWP, and hence would be ushered in as prime minister if his party were to win a majority of the 17 electoral district seats on offer and Chastanet were to win his seat.

It was an intriguing question because at the time of the general elections St. Lucia was only 178 years, or about two (2.35) average St. Lucian lifetimes (St. Lucia life expectancy at birth[1] was 75.75 years in 2016) removed from slavery, and its population was about 85% Black but only 0.6 percent White. Yet the racial composition of the population would be even more skewed toward Blacks than suggested by the 85% if one were to follow America's definition of Black, for according to 2010 St. Lucia population estimates,[2,3,4] 85.3% of the population was African/Black, 10.8 percent was a mix of African and European, 2.2% percent East Indian, 0.6% white, 0.6% Carib, and the remaining 0.5% was 0.1% Chinese, 0.1% Middle Eastern, and 0.3% other or unidentified. Therefore, based on the American definition of Black, at least 96.1% of the population is black, while only 0.6% is white. At least, because a good percentage of the East Indian and Carib population would be mixed with people of African descent.

The question probably held just as much intrigue as: would America elect a black president, back in 2008 after Barack Obama had won the Democratic presidential nomination? And as much intrigue as: would America elect a woman president in the person of Hillary Clinton, albeit one with plenty of political baggage, after Clinton had won her party's 2016 presidential nomination?

However, with Barack Obama, one could understand White Americans temporarily suppressing or suspending their racial prejudices to vote for a black man because he had proven to be outstanding in intellect, integrity, and leadership. Likewise, by virtue of Hillary Clinton's smartness, policy making prowess, and the extensive and varied political offices she had held, making her arguably the best qualified US presidential candidate in history, one could well imagine her overcoming America's remaining reservoir of sexism and the Clintons' political baggage to win the elections. But what extraordinary qualities did Allen Chastanet possess and what distinguished career had he led that would allow the overwhelmingly black population to catch a bout of amnesia and elect a white prime minister?

4

A QUESTION OF FITNESS

The question whether St. Lucia would elect a white prime minister was perhaps even more intriguing than would America elect a black president or would America elect a woman president, because, unlike Barack Obama and Hillary Clinton, other than that Allen Chastanet was paler than most of his fellow countrymen and was born with a silver spoon, to many he did not exactly stand out. In fact, before he entered politics, most St. Lucians hardly knew of him. He had lost the only elections he had contested, and considering his inherited privileges, there was nothing spectacular about his resume.

But that is not to say his bio[1,2] was shabby. He held an undergraduate degree from Bishop's University in Quebec and a master's degree from the American University in Washington, D.C. He served as a tourism director under Sir John Compton's 1992 UWP government, he also served as vice president of marketing and sales for Air Jamaica, president of the St. Lucia Hotel and Tourism Association, chairman of the marketing committee for the Caribbean Hotel Association, director on the board of the ICC Cricket World Cup West Indies 2007, and minister of tourism in

Stephenson King's UWP administration (2006-2011). He is a co-founder of the Caribbean Media Exchange and was involved with the management of two apparently successful and award-winning family-owned hotel properties—Coco Kreole and Coco Palm—in Rodney Bay, Gros Islet, St. Lucia's tourism mecca.

Clearly, on paper, even after one made a discount considering that his whiteness and family connections had opened doors for him, Chastanet did not appear to be the worst among those who had aspired to the prime minister's seat. However, to many of his countrymen, particularly those of the opposing SLP, not only was he not outstanding, his intellect, professional reputation, and achievements were incompatible with national leadership. His detractors referred to him as an empty head lacking substance, such that they questioned his claim of possessing college degrees. They said he could talk a good game but was nothing but a salesman, a con artist. His opponents also regarded him as an inept spend-thrift, incapable of taking care of business. As proof, they point to Air Jamaica's allegedly parting ways with him as vice president of marketing and sales because they said he had run the airline to the ground. They said his father once sacked him as managing director of his hotel because his alleged mismanagement of money had turned the business downhill. It is said that as minister of tourism in the previous UWP administration, he irresponsibly racked up tens of thousands of dollars in phone bills.

Chastanet had another knock against him. In the heat of the 2016 general election campaign, St. Lucian University of the West Indies (UWI) political scientist, Dr. Tennyson Joseph, wrote: "The son of a wealthy businessman, he (Allen Chastanet) does not speak the native vernacular, and his political involvement has coincided with a hurried crash course in being Lucian."[3]

According to this statement, Chastanet was so out of step with the St. Lucian way of life, St. Lucian culture, that he needed a crash course on how to be St. Lucian. If so, it is fair to question the St. Lucian-ness of Allen Chastanet, not based on race, but based on his affinity with the culture, the people, and the land, and hence his passion and dedication to country. This is not a petty issue, because the extent to which one does not have an affinity with the culture, the people, and the land is the extent to which one is likely to sell out the country.

A closer look at Allen Chastanet's past suggests[4] there were other reasons besides an inability to speak the country's mother tongue to question his familiarity and affinity with St. Lucian culture. When Allen was around four years old, Michael Chastanet moved his family and business headquarters to Puerto Rico. After five years in Puerto Rico, the senior Chastanet relocated his family and business head-quarters a second time, to Miami, Florida. Two and a half years later, the family returned to St. Lucia, where Allen attended the Castries Comprehensive Secondary School and St. Mary's College. Apparently, Allen was having a tough time adjusting to St. Lucia and its school system. So much so, that he said to his father, "Dad, if I am to make something useful with my life, I would like you to find me a school in a more advanced country."[4]

In the slavery and colonial era, not bothering to develop a credible educational system, the plantation class (at least those who could afford it) often sent their offspring overseas to boarding school.[5] Well, following in their footsteps and in response to Allen's disgruntlement, Michael Chastanet enrolled his son at Stanstead College, a Quebec boarding high school catering for grades 7 through 12, where Allen completed his secondary education.

Allen Chastanet stayed in Quebec for his undergraduate degree and then worked at the St. Lucia Central Planning Unit in the ministry of finance and planning for two-and-a-half years before enrolling at American University in Washington, D.C., where he graduated with a master's degree in international business.

All this suggests that the prime minister spent most of his childhood and young adult years outside St. Lucia. And when one considers that after college, he worked either outside the country or primarily in the tourism industry, he likely had had little time and opportunity to enmesh himself in St. Lucian culture and way of life. St. Lucia may seem to him more like his second or third home than his first.

Furthermore, given Michael Chastanet's busy schedule conquering the oceans, his wife, Alice, a national of Ireland, may have been the one primarily raising their children. So all things considered, one can hardly be blamed for concluding that Allen Chastanet was cultured as a white European or a white North American.

Like his father, Allen Chastanet has continued the tradition of Whites sending their children overseas to attend secondary school. On a Canadian television station, he said, "I'm a product of Canada, I did my high school in Canada, I did my university in Canada, both my kids go to school in Canada."[6]

It is understandable that St. Lucian parents would send their children overseas to college, but why would they send them overseas (North America) to secondary school? Is it because the white children are uncomfortable mixing with the rest of the population, or is it to ensure they are culturized White (as North Americans or Europeans)? If the latter, then Allen Chastanet's White and North American culturing may have been not by accident but by design.

Besides race, culture, competency, and intellectual soundness, Chastanet, like John Compton, was accused of being a non-St. Lucian born. The constitution doesn't require that a person be born in St. Lucia to be eligible for the role of prime minister. It stipulates that a citizen born elsewhere is required to reside in St. Lucia for a period of at least 12 months immediately before his or her election to the House of Assembly (from which the prime minister is appointed). Nonetheless, Chastanet's accusers may have grounds for believing he was born outside St. Lucia. According to Michael Chastanet,[4] because of an incompatibility between his blood type and that of his wife's, their children were prone to birth complications. So much so, that their "first-born son died five days after birth." So, with Allen, apparently taking no chances, Michael Chastanet sought the help of doctors in Martinique where his son's life was saved by a "direct blood transfusion through his head." When it came to Feolla, the fourth child and second daughter, Michael Chastanet took even fewer chances. He arranged for his wife to give birth in Boston, where Feolla was born without the birth complications of her siblings.

5

THE CREAM SHALL RISE

The question that begs for an answer is that if Allen Chastanet was by no stretch of the imagination an outstanding or gifted person, was of the politically incorrect race, was not born in St. Lucia, and regarding culture was barely a St. Lucian and as such alienated from the vast majority of the population, how then did he become prime minister? How could the man accused of being unfit to run a hotel be fit to run a country?

How Did Allen Chastanet Become Party Leader?

However, in exploring the factors that led to the improbable result of Allen Chastanet occupying the prime minister's chair, it may be instructive to first examine how he became the leader of the United Workers Party, a prerequisite or necessary step to the prime minister's throne.

In 2004, the then leader of the UWP, Dr. Vaughan Lewis, commissioned a popular poll that revealed 74 percent of the population thought the country was heading in the wrong direction under the Labour government, and 63 percent wanted

John Compton at the helm of the UWP. John Compton, who gave up the prime ministership and retired from politics in midterm (1995), was the first and only premier of St. Lucia and its first prime minister. He had been the supreme leader of the UWP since its formation in 1964 and save for an aborted SLP term (1979-1982) had held the reins of government for an uninterrupted 33 years. Apparently, responding to the poll and smarting from the humiliation of two resounding general election defeats since the retirement of John Compton, in early 2005, as the election campaign cycle drew near, a UWP conference of delegates elected John Compton, now 81 years old, as leader of the party, beating out his opponent Dr. Vaughan Lewis with 265 votes against 135.[1]

Compton's comeback into politics was no doubt greeted with hope by UWP supporters but with derision (about his advanced age and likely incapacity to hold high office) by the Labour Party. Thirty-year-old Menissa Rambally, youngest of the Labour Party ministers and candidates (whose entry into politics at age 21 back in 1997 made her the youngest candidate and the youngest minister in St. Lucia's history), pronounced him a "toothless tiger."[2] However, one suspects there was also an inkling of apprehension by the Labour Party, for many have attributed mythical powers to Compton.

To the great chagrin of Rambally and her Labour Party colleagues, John Compton defied age, logic, and expectations and at 82 led his party to an 11–6 victory, in the process adding to his mythical aura.

However, his regained glory was short-lived. For 13 years, 1984 to 1997, Taiwan, during the reign of the UWP, had enjoyed diplomatic relations with St. Lucia. This changed when the Labour Party gained power in 1997. The perception in political circles that Taiwan was biased towards the UWP and was providing the party with financial support must have been a sore point with SLP operators. Moreover, both the prime minister,

Dr. Kenny Anthony, and the minister for foreign affairs, George Odlum, were known communist sympathizers and to have had close ties with Cuba's Fidel Castro. So much so, that in anticipation of SLP's return to power, George Odlum had apparently established ties with the Chinese Ambassador in New York during his stint (1995-1996) as St. Lucia's Ambassador at the United Nations under the John Compton UWP administration. Therefore, it was no surprise when, through the concerted efforts of the foreign minister, St. Lucia switched its diplomatic relations from the Republic of China (Taiwan) to the Communist People's Republic of China.[3]

When Compton's UWP returned to power in 2006, the government was apparently under pressure to re-establish diplomatic relations with the Republic of China (Taiwan). It was rumored that Taiwan had helped finance the party's campaign and had given each minister or elected district representative a substantial sum of money supposedly for the reinstatement of its diplomatic relations. Notwithstanding, it seems that in sorting out what was best for the country, Compton, to the great dismay of many of his Cabinet ministers, considered continuing diplomatic relations with the People's Republic of China. According to the media, in a meeting of the Cabinet, eight of the eleven elected ministers/district representatives staged a rebellions confrontation against the prime minister over his apparent change of heart. Meantime, the foreign minister, Rufus Bousquet, to the apparent displeasure of Compton, signed an agreement with Taiwan officially establishing diplomatic relations. Following these events, John Compton, who just two weeks earlier had had the stamina and fortitude to deliver a four-hour nonstop budget presentation, succumbed to a series of strokes that culminated in his death on September 7, 2007, a mere nine months after he was sworn in as prime minister.[4,5]

However, Compton had time to reshuffle his Cabinet before his death. He appointed Stephenson King to replace him as prime minister and dismissed Rufus Bousquet from Cabinet.

With the death of Compton and the appointment of Stephenson King as prime minister, the UWP administration became a dysfunctional government. King was a weak prime minister. His legitimacy as prime minister was tenuous. He was a prime minister by default; he hadn't gained his position by leading his party into general elections. Besides being a long-time party member and possessing an ability to win his constituency seat, he was undistinguished. Secondary school was apparently his highest level of formal education.[6] He spoke and presented himself in a manner suggestive of a statesman, but his speeches usually lacked substance and cogency. As a weak leader, to keep his position and administration intact, King was forced into compromises. Under pressure from his Cabinet, he dismissed economic planning minister, Ausbert D'Auvergne, a highly praised economic management guru whom Compton had appointed, and returned Rufus Bousquet, whom Compton had sacked, to Cabinet.

For a while it seemed government ministers were spending more time under police arrest than in Cabinet. Richard Frederick, minister for housing, urban renewal, and local government, whose entry into politics Kenny Anthony reportedly characterized as "the most frightening prospect" of St. Lucian politics, was arrested for alleged tax evasion and under-invoicing on his car imports.[7] Following an article[8] by Rick Wayne suggesting that a prominent St. Lucian politician may be a convicted US felon who once went by the alias "Bruce Duane Tucker", Rufus Bousquet was forced to confess[9] that he was the "Bruce Tucker" of Rick Wayne's article and that in his twenties he was arrested in the US and convicted of passport fraud and sentenced to 40 hours of community service and two years probation. Moreover, for reasons undisclosed, the U.S. State Department cancelled Richard Frederick's diplomatic visa.[10] One got the impression that the UWP was an administration of convicts and drug traffickers.

Apparently, the absence of a strong prime minister gave rise to a power vacuum, and so it seemed every minister, irrespective of ability and qualifications, spread his wings to fill the vacuum. A phenomenon that gave the impression that every minister was a prime minister unto himself. Hence it appeared that St. Lucia had eleven prime ministers running the country, and in any week it was anyone's guess who would posture as prime minister.

In this atmosphere of dysfunctionality, besides its alleged campaign financing and purchasing of diplomatic relations, the Taiwanese government corrupted the government system. It handed cash to individual ministers and district constituencies as part of government aid, further destabilizing the government, exacerbating its dysfunctionality, and buttressing the notion every minister was a government unto himself. The Taiwanese ambassador, Tom Chou, was so in-your-face and so much part of the politics of the country, that he attracted more heat from the calypsonians than did ministers of government. In effect, he became yet another prime minister of St. Lucia's multiple prime ministers. So much was Tom Chou a part of the governing of the country that, long after he had returned to his country, Minister Guy Joseph could not help but comment in his 2016 election victory speech that the UWP victory was a vote for Tom Chou.[11]

So then what does all this have to do with Allen Chastanet gaining the leadership of his party?

In the 2006 general elections, Chastanet had not contested a seat but taking advantage of his tourism expertise, John Compton in his great wisdom ignored possible conflict of interest (Chastanet was managing director of twin hotels) and appointed him as a senator and minister for tourism. It is not clear whether Compton's appointment of Chastanet was just for his tourism experience or that he also saw Chastanet as prime minister material and the appointment was the start of that process. What was clear is despite naysayers' misgivings about Chastanet's abilities, Compton had confidence in him. After all, in a previous administration he had appointed Chastanet as director of tourism. When Compton fell ill in 2007 after the mutinous confrontation with his Cabinet ministers, he could not have appointed Chastanet as his replacement because Chastanet was a non-elected Cabinet minister and he was relatively a newcomer to the party and to politics.

In the post-Compton dysfunctional UWP administration, Allen Chastanet was one of the few bright lights. He was untarnished by the alleged Taiwanese induced corruption, for he hadn't gone up for elections and so did not require Taiwanese campaign funds and he was ineligible for any Taiwanese diplomatic relations' bribe money because as a non-voting/non-elected Cabinet minister he did not have a say in such diplomatic decisions. And as a non-elected Cabinet minister, he could not have been part of the group of Cabinet ministers who had rebelled against Compton over the question of Taiwanese diplomatic relations and which had precipitated his death. Furthermore, among the ministers who postured as prime minister (King included), Chastanet seemed the most articulate, the most capable, and the most knowledgeable and proactive in his area of ministership. Chastanet appeared the most prime ministerial.

General elections came along in 2011 and given the weak leadership, corruption, and the dysfunctionality of the Stephenson King-led UWP administration, no one was surprised when the Labour Party under the helm of Dr. Kenny Anthony returned to power with an 11-6 majority. In this election, Allen Chastanet had contested the Soufriere seat, an obvious move given that Soufriere was one of the two districts (the other being Gros Islet) most dependent on tourism, and Chastanet was seen as a tourism guru. Chastanet lost the elections, but he had received a baptism in St. Lucian politics.

With a defeat at the polls and the UWP in disarray, there was need for an organizational shakeup, need for a change in leadership. Some of the more obvious leadership choices of the party included Lenard Montoute, Stephenson King, Rufus Bousquet, and Richard Frederick. Regarding Lenard Montoute and Stephenson King, not only were they two of the most senior UWP parliamentarians but as the only two (elected) Cabinet ministers who stood on the side of Compton during the confrontation that had hastened his demise, the country did not see them as having the blood of Compton on their hands. Rufus Bousquet and Richard Frederick represented a different story. Both had at least two strikes against them. First, they were among the group of mutinous Cabinet ministers. Second, thanks to Rick Wayne and to US passport fraud, Rufus Bousquet was perceived as a convicted US criminal with a history of hiding his true identity; and regarding Richard Frederick, the United States cancellation of his diplomatic visa placed him in such bad light that by September 2011 he was forced to resign as Cabinet minister.[12]

As for Allen Chastanet, although he had given a good account of himself as minister of tourism in Stephenson King's dysfunctional administration, and compared to some of his colleagues he had remained untainted, he must have been viewed as a political novice, a Compton experiment, a foreigner of the politically incorrect race, who was yet to successfully contest an election, and therefore a non-threat to the leadership of the party. But in politics, as in life, image and perception can go a long way.

Allen Chastanet surprised many (probably none more so than King and Montoute who probably thought the party leadership was their birthright since, after all, King had been party leader and prime minister and Montoute had been deputy prime minister) when not once, but thrice he successfully contested the party leadership at annual party conventions. First in 2013 against Stephenson King, then in 2014 against economist Dr. Claudius Preville, and then in 2015 against lawyer Sarah Flood Beaubrun.

Apparently, the Chastanet pill was too bitter or too big for King and Montoute to swallow. They took to the sidelines where they apparently continued to attack Chastanet's capacity to lead the party to election victory. However, one suspects that their real beef was that they viewed Chastanet as barely a St. Lucian, a charlatan, an upstart propped up by his father's reputation and wealth who hadn't paid his dues and so undeserving of the leadership position he had wrestled from under their very noses. In their eyes his legitimacy as the leader of the party and as the possible prime minister of the country was suspect.

However, Chastanet went further than just winning his party's top position. In August 2014, Frederick was expelled from the party. With that move, all challengers to Chastanet's leadership were sidelined or cut off. The charismatic and combative Richard Frederick, who had (what one suspects) his prime ministership aspirations aborted by the US withdrawal of his diplomatic visa, did not take his expulsion lightly. Turning into a talk show host, he used his show and any other platform at his disposal to lambaste the prime minister. Not unlike when Dr. Kenny Anthony had ousted Rick Wayne, St. Lucia's world-renowned bodybuilder and the island's most famous journalist, from the Senate; and since then Rick Wayne has used his newspaper column and television talk show to criticize the three-term prime minister at every turn.

With this and other maneuverings, Chastanet hinted that under his leadership the UWP had been modernized and strengthened and therefore in much better shape to contest the next elections and govern the country. This view was optimistic at best, because Chastanet did not have a clear road ahead. The road ahead was rocky and thorny. The party was apparently split between the King faction and the Chastanet faction. So much so that when the June 2016 election was called, giving the UWP only a few weeks advanced notice, it was not clear that the party could field 17 credible contestants. Two stalwarts of the party, Stephenson King and Lenard Montoute, remained at loggerheads with Chastanet and showed no signs of throwing their hat in the ring. Nightly, Richard Frederick was on the airwaves desperately trying to make sure Chastanet's bid for the prime ministership remained but a dream.

Nonetheless, Chastanet had taken the penultimate step to the prime ministership, and sometimes no matter how farfetched some dreams come true.

6

AGAINST ALL ODDS

How Did Allen Chastanet Become Prime Minister?

B ack to the question that begs for an answer. How did Allen Chastanet, a non-St. Lucian born, a political novice of the politically incorrect race, who many saw as lacking the capacity for the job, who culturally speaking was barely a St. Lucian, and whose political party was dysfunctional and in disarray, lead his party to election victory, in the process gaining the throne? The answer is manifold.

The Ambition Factor

Everyone, including the opposition party and the likes of King, Montoute, and Frederick, seemed to have underestimated the fortitude, ambition, and capabilities of Allen Chastanet. After the elections, Chastanet acquaintances revealed that since his college days he had prophesied he would be prime minister of St. Lucia. On September 19, 2016, just three months after winning the elections, Chastanet gave a 90-minute press conference that made a liar of those who said he was an empty head. The prime minister was calm, poised, collected, and stately. He answered all questions thoughtfully, substantively, and forthrightly. Even when a question had several parts, he remembered all the parts and answered each. And sometime later, in a television interview on the subject of government borrowing upwards of EC$100 million from the St. Lucia National Insurance Corporation (which serves as a national pension fund) to process government bonds about to come due on the regional government securities market (RGSM), while economist, Dr. Ubaldus Raymond, minister in the ministry of finance, was inarticulate and seemingly befuddled, Chastanet was fluent, self-assured, and provided clear, concise answers. One got the impression that it was Chastanet and not Dr. Ubaldus who held the PhD in economics. From all appearances, the prime minister was not the airhead that some had made him out to be. In both instances, he handled himself as well as any head of government.

Interestingly, while SLP stalwarts kept bombarding voters with the unfitness of Chastanet to rule, there was evidence that the populace was not overly impressed with their rhetoric. A poll conducted by Caribbean Development Research Services (CADRES) just weeks before the elections had pronounced the results of the elections too close to call and its finding that 31% of respondents preferred to be led by Kenny Anthony and 28% by Allen Chastanet suggested there was not much separating the leaders in terms of voter preference.[1]

In terms of ambition, one senses that Allen Chastanet did not just want to be prime minister, he was aiming at nothing less than to replicate and even surpass Sir John's colossal political accomplishments. And Chastanet could point to some similarities he shared with Compton. They were of similar skin tone. They were not born on St. Lucian soil—Chastanet was supposedly born on the French island of Martinique, Compton said he was born in Canouan, one of the Grenadine islands situated between St. Vincent and Grenada, but as a child he spent a lot of time in St. Lucia, and at eleven settled there for good.[2] Compton was of a seafaring people, Chastanet's father began compiling his fortune as a boatbuilder and operator of ocean-going vessels.

Notwithstanding the similarities Chastanet shared with Compton, he was facing the predicament of all sons who grew up in the shadows of a famously successful father. How does one become one's own man, how does one forge one's own identity, how does one supplant, surpass, a legend?

In Law 41 (avoid stepping into a great man's shoes) of the international bestselling book, *The 48 Laws of Power*,[3] Robert Greene may have provided the answer to this dilemma. He said:

> What happens first always appears better and more original than what comes after. If you succeed a great man or have a famous parent, you will have to accomplish double their achievements to outshine them. Do not get lost in their shadow, or stuck in a past not of your own making: establish your own name and identity by changing course. Slay the overbearing father, disparage his legacy, and gain power by shining in your own way.

Well it seems for a while there Chastanet was following in his father's footsteps, in his father's shadow, managing his father's hotels, but apparently this was not working too well for him. So as if following Robert Greene's suggestion he changed course, took a different path, entered politics, knowing that in politics he could go where his father could only dream of, or the closest his father could get was to bankroll elections, write news paper articles, and host talk shows. Thus in politics Chastanet could make a name for himself, cultivate a legacy distinct from that of his father.

At first Michael Chastanet was not happy about his son's involvement in politics. He wanted his son to take after him and continue and advance the family's business legacy. In his memoir,[4] which seemed designed to clean up his legacy and enhance his son's public image, the senior Chastanet said that he had discouraged his son from accepting John Compton's offer to serve as minister of tourism and aviation in Compton's 2006 government; and after Compton's demise and the ensuing dysfunctionality of the UWP government, he had repeatedly advised his son to resign from government; and again, after his son had lost his bid for the Soufriere seat in the 2011 general elections, he had begged him to leave politics alone. Obviously, Allen Chastanet did not heed his father's admonitions. Not when politics offered him a means of stepping out of his father's shadow and become his own man, gain his own identity, establish his own legacy.

On second thought, it seems that Dr. Kenny Anthony had taken to heart Robert Greene's suggestion even more deeply than did Allen Chastanet. Not so much by taking a different course, but by disparaging Compton's legacy and zealously pursuing large construction projects as if to outdo Compton and in the process erect his own legacy, his own monuments. But as Robert Greene said, it is difficult to outshine a great man by continuing in his traditions. One may well outdo him in accomplishments, but there is something to be said about being the first, being mythical, being a colossus in people's eyes. Some would argue that regarding George Odlum Dr. Kenny Anthony also appeared to have taken some pointers from *48 Laws of Power*, but in Odlum's case he attempted to do so by taking a different path, pursuing a pragmatic, centrist political path to Odlum's left of center political stance, in the process acquiring the fresh identity of "New Labour". Both Compton and Odlum are no longer with us, and Kenny Anthony, who some would argue overstayed his political welcome, is apparently in the weaning years of his political career, so one wonders how the St.

Lucian public would rank the relative greatness of these three men. In 2005, The Jako Magazine carried an article, "St. Lucia Men of the Century: Sir George Charles, Sir John Compton, and George Odlum"[5,6]. If the magazine was writing that article today, would it include Kenny Anthony as a candidate for Man of the Century?

The Slogan Factor

Pollsters and political scientists may have overlooked a critical predictor of election outcomes. For it appears that the party or candidate with the most catchy and compelling campaign slogans usually wins the election. Slogans that resonate with voters, and that capture the public's imagination. Let's look at a few examples.

Ronald Reagan (1980) *Let's Make America Great Again.* Ronald Reagan (1984) *It's Morning Again in America.* George Bush (1988) *Kinder, Gentler Nation; Read My Lips, No New Taxes.* Bill Clinton (1992) *It's Time to Change America; It's the Economy, Stupid.* Bill Clinton (1996) *Building a Bridge to the Twenty-first Century.* Barack Obama (2008) *Hope.* Barack Obama (2012) *Forward.* Donald Trump (2016) *Make America Great Again.* St. Lucia Labour Party (2011) *En Rouge,* In Red. St. Lucia United Workers Party (2016) *Yo Pè,* They Afraid.

In the 2011 general elections, *En Rouge* seemed to have crowded out all other sounds, all other voices, and to have impassioned, galvanized voters and party members into action. One had the impression that the entire island was colored red. Then in 2016, it seemed that *Yo Pè* was all one heard, and one had the impression that SLP supporters were scuttling for cover, and the island was painted yellow.

It seems that the party with the most self-belief, the party most in tune with the mood of voters, and with momentum on its side is the one most likely to come up with the slogan that would resonate with voters and capture their imagination. And the slogan helps build momentum, creates its own magic, takes on a life of its own.

If so, will the SLP slogan *Chastanet-must-go* do the trick for Labour in the up and coming elections? Only time will tell. But Chastanet and the UWP would do well to come up with a slogan of their own. Maybe, *Chastanet-must-stay*.

The Race Factor or rather The Colorism Factor

During the election campaign the Labour Party made half-hearted attempts to make political fodder of the fact that Chastanet was a white man (or an almost white man), seeking to be the prime minister of a predominantly black country and, to add insult to injury, he was not even conversant in Kwéyòl, the people's mother tongue, signaling he was not *okouwan* with the country's culture. One suspects that out of desperation the Labour Party was trying to make the campaign a race issue. But they got it all wrong and were no more successful using the race issue against Chastanet than they were some decades ago using the country of birth issue against Sir John Compton, whom they had claimed was born in St. Vincent or on the Caribbean channel between St. Vincent and St. Lucia. In fact, by drawing attention to Chastanet's whiteness, they may have inadvertently helped him win the elections.

They should have realized that it was not an accident that since when Sir George F.L. Charles served as chief minister (1960-1964), the only persons who have run an election as leader of his party and in the process headed the government for a full term are those regarded as either half-white or almost white. It is a shortlist. Sir John Compton, Dr. Kenny Anthony, and now Allen Chastanet. And to this list it would be remiss of one not to add Learie Carasco, renamed Rick Wayne, who as a prime minister maker is the closest one has gotten to being prime minister without ever running for office. It would appear that being light on melanin is a good start to becoming the prime minister of St. Lucia. If so, the Labour Party might be on the right track in grooming Dr. Ernest Hilaire, former CEO of West Indies Cricket Board and former St. Lucia High Commissioner to the United Kingdom, for the party leadership and hence the prime ministership. In terms of electability, the current party leader, Philip J. Pierre, as a candidate for prime minister, may be a non-starter.

The legacy of slavery and white colonialism and imperialism are manifest. In St. Lucia, parents favor their lighter skin children over their darker skin ones; skin tone discrimination starts right there in the home. Children quickly learn that because of their darker skin they are worth less than their lighter skin siblings or cousins. In parents' verbal abuse of their children, or in general when people are quarreling with each other, their blackness is fair game. The nation's language is replete with self-hatred: *neg mize'wab*, niggers are miserable; *neg mové*, niggers are wicked; *neg modi*, niggers are cursed; *sé kon sa nou neg yé*, that is how we niggers are; *ou nwè kon kaka kochon*, you're black as pig's shit.

How many times have one listened to one's fellow St. Lucians describe someone whom they thought was attractive as "the good-looking boy/girl with nice skin (light complexion) and good hair (straight hair)?" It isn't so long ago when most of the women working as bank tellers fitted the description of "fair skin" and "nice hair."

Sadly, many place a premium on whiteness. It has been ingrained that white is superior to black. To be white is to be more valuable, more important. The presence of white people at an event gives weight and legitimacy to it. When a white person speaks, one pays greater attention. It is easier for white people or for half-white people than it is for dark skin St. Lucians to get bank loans, to get their business proposals taken seriously, to get an audience with prime ministers and other leaders of government and industry.

Apparently, this phenomenon is not unique to St. Lucia. There is a world-wide valuation of Whites versus non-Whites. Everywhere one goes, even after controlling for education and income, compared to Blacks, Whites enjoy better housing, live in environmentally sounder neighborhoods, have access to better healthcare and education, and have better access to the factors of production. There is a premium on whiteness. It seems black people have no true homes. Overseas they are third or fourth class citizens, and at home they are at best second-class citizens.

Donald Trump has Barack Obama to thank for his presidency. For America reasoned if a black man can be president, then any white man, no matter how disgusting, how retarded, can be president. And as if to signal to African Americans that it was no big deal having a black president, they side-stepped the most qualified US presidential candidate in history in the person of Hillary Clinton to elect Donald Trump, the least qualified one in history.

The Labour Party should have taken a page from the likes of Flow, Digicel and other commercial houses. Because they clearly understand the appeal to St. Lucian consumers of whiteness relative to blackness. For it seems that their advertisements are disproportionately populated with lighter skin models.

It is ironic, though, that by jumping on the boat with Kenny Anthony the Labour Party had ridden the wave of whiteness to win three out of the last four administrative terms, yet there they were trying to use the whiteness issue against the UWP. Well, it turned out the whiter candidate won the race.

In an interview[7] on MBC Television St. Lucia, Dr. Kenny Anthony alluded to comments by Allen Chastanet suggesting he was not born with the name Anthony but had changed his name from Barnard, his father's surname, to Anthony, his mother's surname, to make himself more acceptable to the St. Lucian public. He also indicated that he was aware that some of his detractors were referring to him as "Massa" in reference to the accusation he was a descendent of slave masters. It is understandable why St. Lucians would link Kenny Anthony to slave masters, because right up to the late 1950s his grandfather, Dennis Barnard, was the owner and operator of the Dennery estates and sugar factories. It was at one of these factories, during the 1957 sugar strike, that the legendary incident occurred involving John Compton as an advocate of workers facing off with Dennis Barnard, each pulling out their guns.[8] The event portrayed Compton as the hero, the David, who stood up to Goliath, the evil "Massa". It added a feather to his mythical aura and effectively launched his political career.

With so much attached to such a powerful and negative connotation, the former prime minister took pains to explain that nothing can be further from the truth. He said that he had never hidden the fact that he was the illegitimate son of his parents, and illegitimate children were usually given the name of their mothers'. He admitted that his brothers changed their names to Barnard, but at no time had he contemplated or attempted to change his name. On the contrary, he was proud of his mother and proud to carry her name. So much so, that he dedicated his doctoral thesis to her. Dr. Anthony also said that what was ironic about this accusation was that several years ago he had discovered that his surname should not have been Anthony, which was the first name of his maternal grandfather, so his mother was mistakenly given her father's Christian name as her surname. Regarding his Barnard roots, he said the Barnards first came to the Caribbean from Sussex, England, in the 1880s, long after slavery was over, so they could not have been involved in St. Lucian slavery. Some went into agriculture by purchasing failing estates, and some others went into commerce.

So apparently based on who were descendants of slave masters, Kenny Anthony would win the argument hands down.

The irony of this jostling for position to either link the other to slave-owing ancestors or to dispel any doubt of their ancestors' involvement in slavery is that if slave ownership ancestry was the basis for determining which St. Lucians care about the well-being of their country or which St. Lucians were fit to be prime minister, then many St. Lucians whom the census classifies as of African descent and who may be as black as people can be would fail the test, because according to Dr. Jolien Harmsen et al.,[9] many blacks and colored St. Lucians owned slaves and sugar plantations. For example, the authors reported that in 1828 there were about 5000 free colored and black people in St. Lucia; they owned 2350 slaves (1202 plantation slaves and 1148 personal slaves), or about one-sixth of the slave population.

Besides the intriguing question of whether St. Lucia would elect a white prime minister, it was amazing that other than the Labour politicians and party hacks, the topic received little attention, as if it was a non-issue. Few journalists mentioned it, the population hardly mentioned it. When the topic came up, some people's reaction was: "Well, Chastanet is not fully white"; or "Well, if racist America can elect a black president, why can't St. Lucia elect a white prime minister?"

Interesting analogies. But there are differences. Black or African Americans comprise about 13 percent of the US population, while Whites form only 0.6 percent of the St. Lucia population; therefore, all else being equal, it should be easier for the US to elect a black president than St. Lucia to elect a white prime minister.

US national or federal elections comprise senatorial, house representative, and presidential elections. In contrast, St. Lucia has just one election, which involves electing district representatives, and the party that wins the most seats is invited to form the government, and the leader of that party, assuming that he won his seat, usually, though not automatically, becomes prime minister. So whereas in the US the population cast presidential votes, in St. Lucia the population do not vote for a prime minister, but vote for their district representatives. Therefore, it is a misnomer to say that St. Lucians elected a white prime minister. They elected the UWP, and it so happened the UWP was headed by a white district representative. Thus, regarding the electoral process, it would be easier for a white person to become the prime minister of St. Lucia than a black person to become the US president, because in St. Lucia voters are not confronted directly with a choice between a white and a black prime minister candidate.

The choice between a white and a black candidate only occurred in Micoud South, where Chastanet contested the constituency seat, and not the prime minister position. Therefore, if the Labour Party wanted to blame someone for allowing a white man to become prime minister (assuming this is a desirable goal), they need look no further than Micoud South, which takes the narrative to the Desruisseaux factor.

The Desruisseaux Factor

Situated in the southeast of St. Lucia, and sandwiched between Vieux Fort North and Dennery South, and stretching from the Caribbean Sea to the central interior of the island, Micoud is the third largest of St. Lucia's ten districts both in terms of land area (30 sq. miles) and population (16,284).[10] It is home to some of the island's most productive agricultural lands, and its dense rain forest is populated with the Amazona versicolor (the St. Lucian Parrot), St. Lucia's national bird, and with a variety of hardwood timber, including mahogany, used for furniture, and gommier, used to make traditional fishing pirogues called *canots.*

Micoud is also John Compton and UWP country. Beginning in 1954 when John Compton first entered politics, Micoud (or Dennery-Micoud) was the only seat he ever contested, which he never lost, and since the formation of the UWP in 1964, only once did the UWP lose a Micoud seat, and that was in Micoud South in 1997 when the Labour Party swept into power by a landslide that left only one UWP seat standing — Micoud North.

In the previous election (2011), Chastanet had contested the Soufriere seat, which, as pointed out earlier, made sense given his hotel experience and the town's overwhelming dependence on tourism. However, this was always going to be a risky proposition because of the 12 elections that had been held since the formation of the UWP, the party had won the Soufriere seat only four times, and the last time was in 1992.[11]

In 2016 Chastanet got smart, or he followed excellent advice. He opted for the Micoud (Micoud South) seat, which, as mentioned earlier, the UWP had lost only once in its 52-year history or 12-election-cycle history. There was only one slight problem. The seat was occupied by an entrenched UWP stalwart, Arsene James, an educator and former minister of education and culture, who had been occupying the seat for nearly 15 years or three terms. A humble, soft-spoken, low key personality, Arsene James seemed more at home in his home village of Desruisseaux, playing dominoes with the boys and looking after his community, than in parliament with all its grandstanding. Therefore, already in his seventies and having endured two careers (educator and politician), Allen Chastanet probably did not have to try too hard to convince Arsene James to step down for the good of the party, especially since, according to rumors, the deal came with substantial financial incentives for Arsene James.

Desruisseaux, a rural hamlet at the heart of Micoud South, can be regarded as the capital of the electoral district (St. Lucia has ten districts, but for election purposes, the island is divided into 17 constituencies or electoral districts). Desruisseaux, where it has been said that the James family is the closest thing to royalty, is a prosperous and progressive community.

Desruisseauxnians are a prideful people who think highly of themselves and who socially punch above their weight, or hang their hats higher than their reach. Sir Dunstan St. Omer, a cultural hero, and the designer of the national flag, once said that St. Lucians are an aristocratic people, they have *lògèy*[12] (pride). One wonders if he had Desruisseaux in mind when he made that pronouncement. For such a people, economic benefits aside, it would be a feather in their cap to have the prime minister of the country as their district representative. It would be a great boost to their ego, it would put Desruisseaux on the map. Consider this, of all the prime ministers of St. Lucia, it is only Allen Chastanet whose constituency does not encompass or is not part of a district center. Micoud South does not overlap or intersect with the Village of Micoud. As Micoud South district rep, Allen Chastanet represents rural St. Lucia.

Considering all this, Allen Chastanet opting to contest Micoud South was a stroke of genius, for he chose the very people most likely to overlook his skin color for the opportunity to house a prime minister. But maybe Desruisseaux did not overlook his race at all, on the contrary, if St. Lucians place a premium on whiteness, then having an almost white prime minister would be even a larger feather in Desruisseaux's cap, the rural hamlet would have one-upped Vieux Fort. As SLP found out, albeit too late, whoever underestimates Chastanet does so at their own peril.

The Kenny Anthony Factor

A few months after the 2016 general elections, a prominent Vieux Fort businessman and a strong supporter of SLP said that it was Labour supporters' fault that the party had lost the elections. SLP supporters took too much of a back seat. They did not go out and enthusiastically campaign and support the party.

One can well imagine a Vieux Fortian responding to this statement with: *Come on, you know very well that people (Vieux Fortians, especially) were disappointed with Kenny Anthony and the SLP. Kenny and company have no one to blame but themselves. They let a party defeat them, which in the 2011 elections voters had soundly rejected, not least because of its disintegration into a dysfunctional government that had proven unfit to govern, a party that had probably set the country back ten, fiften years, a party that just weeks before the elections was in disarray.*

So then what did Dr. Kenny Anthony and SLP do or did not do that paved the road to Chastanet gaining control of government? Well, for a full picture, it will help to briefly trace the history of the Kenny Anthony SLP.

A brief history. In 1993, protesting low banana prices and corruption in the St. Lucia Banana Growers Association (SLBGA) that was supposed to be safeguarding their interest, banana farmers went on a banana no-cut strike, barricading roads, bringing the country to a standstill. When the then prime minister, John Compton, could not take it anymore, after all he himself had driven through an inferno of burning tires engineered by striking farmers to prevent safe passage, he commanded the police to take any action necessary to bring the lawlessness to an end. Following the prime minister's command, the police shot dead two farmers in the Mabouya Valley, thus ending the strike and bringing to a close a sordid chapter in St. Lucia's history.[13]

Two years following the 1993 island-wide banana strike, as if sensing the unforgiving mood of the country, Compton stepped down as prime minister and gave the helm of government to Dr. Vaughan Lewis, who would contest the 1997 general elections as leader of the UWP.

It was then that Kenny Anthony, the minister of education under the failed 1979 SLP government who, in the middle of the SLP debacle, had sought sanctuary at the University of the West Indies, returned home much like Moses in the House of Pharaoh or Joseph in the land of Egypt, to take over the leadership of the SLP.

With many St. Lucians viewing Dr. Kenny Anthony as the Messiah who would help break Compton and UWP's political stranglehold, who would modernize the country and lead it boldly and prosperously into the information age, John Compton's experiment of Vaughan Lewis as his successor failed miserably. The 1997 general elections swept Kenny Anthony and his Labour Party into power by a 16-1 landslide victory, to be followed by another landslide victory of 14-3 in 2001.

As the 2006 elections drew near, probably dismayed and embarrassed that the party he had spent most of his professional life building had become the joke of the nation, losing two consecutive elections by landslides, Compton, as has been noted, wrenched the party leadership from Dr. Vaughan Lewis at a party convention leadership contest to become the one to lead the UWP in the 2006 general elections.

For its part, having won the two previous general elections by landslides and facing a geriatric John Compton, the SLP was no doubt smugly confident that a third term was a forgone conclusion. So much so that as mentioned earlier Menissa Rambally, the youngest in their midst who was barely three years old when Compton had led the country into independence, had had the audacity to call the father of the nation a "toothless tiger."

Understandably, disgusted with Compton's betrayal, Dr. Vaughan Lewis crossed over to the Labour Party under which he would contest for an electoral seat. All this suggested that the UWP was a troubled party, and ill-prepared to contest general elections, and thus should have been minced meat for the SLP, which explained its smugness and election confidence.

Kenny Anthony and the SLP had still more reasons to feel invincible. One accusation against Compton's rule was that he focused on economic and infrastructural development to the neglect of social and people development. Another accusation was that non-UWP voting communities were often neglected in terms of such basic infrastructure as roads, water, and electricity. Consequently, when Dr. Anthony came into power in 1997, he found many rural communities in darkness and without running water, police stations and health centers crumbling and inadequate, highways and urban areas poorly lit, and though nearly twenty years into independence large numbers of eligible students could not attend secondary school because of insufficient classroom space. In sharp contrast, and as if waving a magic wand, Dr. Kenny Anthony's administration fostered a kinder and gentler country, providing universal secondary education, bringing electricity, water and telecommunications services to every nook and cranny of the island, renovating or building health centers, police and fire stations, and establishing footpaths and affordable low income land and housing development.

Besides these social infrastructural developments, Dr. Anthony's administration introduced a greater level of discipline, professionalism, accountability and transparency not just to the civil service but also to government, to governing. He moved the country away from the archaic strongman government to a government run by professionals. He truly brought St. Lucia into the twenty-first century. And this is probably what got Compton into trouble when he faced the mutinous Cabinet ministers over the Taiwanese diplomatic issue. As in the old days, Compton probably thought he could make his mind and change his mind at will with little objection from his Cabinet ministers. But having inculcated a more democratic style of governance, Dr. Kenny Anthony had seemingly foiled that play.

Notwithstanding, if SLP had any cause for worry, it was because they had made a few blunders, which by now are all too well known. A quick list of the blunders included the disrespect and denigration of John Compton; the unforgiveness and vindictiveness toward George Odlum; the audacity of attempting to give themselves back pay; the rush to supplant John Compton's legacy by putting up conspicuous structures and monuments without well thought-out plans of how to fully utilize these structures and how they were going to be maintained; the arrogance of signaling a superiority to the people they served; the sense that government ministers were more about the wearing of expensive suits and taking overseas shopping trips than taking care of the business of the country; Dr. Anthony's arrogance and the signaling of indispensability by having party rules changed to allow him to run a third term as party leader; Rochamel, Grynberg and other such government business debacles that suggest business savvy is not one of Kenny Anthony's strengths, thus he would be wise to rely more heavily on his Cabinet and business and financial advisors when brokering such deals or agreements.

Apparently, the negatives outweighed the positives, and led by the mythical but geriatric John Compton, UWP was ushered into power by an 11-6 majority. And for some of the reasons mentioned above, to many St. Lucians the 2006 elections was above all a vote against Dr. Kenny Anthony. But as has been noted, the accosting of John Compton by the mutinous band of eight Cabinet ministers over the Taiwanese diplomacy affair led to his premature death. With Compton's death, the UWP administration degenerated into a dysfunctional government that probably set the country back ten, fifteen years. Under those circumstances no one should have been surprised when SLP returned to power in 2011 with an 11-6 majority.

During the campaign leading to the 2011 elections, Dr. Anthony was humble and contrite. *He had heard the people loud and clear. He had gotten it.* However, it was never clear what he had gotten. But nothing is more humbling and humiliating than defeat, especially when one did not see it coming, and especially defeat at the hands of a geriatric senior citizen, a "toothless tiger," regardless of his supposed supernatural powers.

Notwithstanding, Dr. Kenny Anthony and the SLP returned to power with their hands full. Before charging forward, they had to undo the damage caused by a dysfunctional UWP administration.

First, there were the Black Bay lands. The UWP government had swapped 469.5 acres of Black Bay and Cannelles lands for shares in the developer Roebuck Properties (St. Lucia), where Roebuck would use the land to establish a five-star Ritz Carlton Resort at Black Bay, along the Vieux Fort-Laborie corridor. Unfortunately, the project went under, forcing the developer to default on the loan of approximately US$25 million it had secured from the Kaupthing Singer & Friedlander bank to finance the resort. Kaupthing Singer & Friedlander collapsed and entered into administration; and, understandably, the administrators, in a hurry to recoup the Roebuck Properties loan, threatened to sell the Black Bay and Cannelles lands, forcing the freshly elected SLP government to come up with the EC$58.72 million required to buy back the lands.[14]

Second, there was the Taiwanese government corrupting the political process and undermining its transparency and accountability by funneling monies directly to district representatives instead of giving the funds to the central government (as required by the Finance Act) to be deposited in a consolidated fund constituted by law with established disbursement procedures. Upon reelection, Dr. Kenny Anthony, who as a matter of principle was one of the few if not the only district rep to refuse the Taiwanese constituency district funds, quickly abolished the practice and reaffirmed the role of the consolidated funds.

Third, there was VAT. By the time Kenny Anthony's Labour Party regained power in 2011, following studies by the IMF (2002) and the OECS Tax Commission (2004) that recommended the implementation of VAT, except St. Lucia, all OECS states had already instituted VAT. The Stephenson King-led UWP administration had toyed with the idea of implementing VAT but apparently shied away because of the potential political fallout. So the thankless task had fallen on Kenny Anthony's Labour government. Fully aware the populace would not take kindly to what they perceived as an additional tax, the prime minister went to great lengths to explain that given the country's debt situation, it had no choice but to implement VAT, which was long overdue. It was either St. Lucia impose economic self-discipline of which VAT was the first step or be subjected to austerity measures under an IMF economic recovery program. VAT was the price the country had to pay to keep the IMF at bay.

Turning its attention to the country's persistently high unemployment, the government reintroduced the Short Term Employment Program (STEP) that it had established in its previous term but which the Stephenson King UWP administration had discontinued. And in 2012 the government launched the National Initiative to Create Employment (NICE), which, among several other unemployment busting measures, included a program that employed single mothers as home caregivers to the elderly. However, the centerpiece of the government's unemployment busting and economic boosting initiative was its construction stimulus package that included lower mortgage rates, and exemption of construction materials from VAT, customs duties, and other government fees.

In the wake of the dysfunctional Stephenson King administration, not only did the SLP government do all this heavy lifting, but continuing the notion of creating a kinder and gentler country, besides NICE and STEP the government established ICT centers in various communities and gave a laptop to every one of the nation's Form Three and Four secondary school students.

Therefore, the question that begs for an answer is that having rescued the country from the misadventures of the Stephenson King UWP government, having undone some of the damage it had created, and then having charged forward to put the country on the path of economic recovery, how could SLP have lost the elections to an opposition party in turmoil, an opposition party that up to three weeks before the elections was not clear of being able to fill a slate of 17 candidates?

There was VAT. In answering this question, the discourse begins with VAT. First, any administration, be it SLP or UWP, that had implemented VAT would have suffered at the polls. Second, whereas it is true that VAT replaced the Environmental Protection Levy, Motor Vehicle Rental Fee, Mobile Cellular Telephone Tax, and the Hotel Accommodation Tax and therefore to some extent could be viewed as a replacement tax, the public viewed VAT as an additional tax, the opposite of what economists would have recommended given that in the aftermath of the Great Recession the country was in the midst of sluggish economic growth and rising unemployment. So even though it was true that VAT was a long overdue necessity, it could not have come at a worse time. Moreover, businesses may have done the government a disfavor. They were supposed to pass on to consumers in the form of reduced prices the reduction in customs fees and other government fees that accompanied VAT, so retail prices should not have risen by the full amount of the VAT. Thus, the extent to which businesses failed to pass on the reduction, was the extent to which consumers bore the full brunt of the VAT.

There were IMPACS and Rick Wayne. During Stephenson King's administration, responding to rising crime in the country, the government unleashed Operation Restore Confidence, and apparently so empowered, police officers, acting as jury, judge and executioner, allegedly conducted several extra-judicial killings during the final year of the UWP administration. The US government responded. In the name of human rights violations, it revoked the visas of some of the top brass of the St. Lucia Police Force, suspended cooperation with St. Lucia on security matters, and threatened further action if St. Lucia did not bring the perpetrators to justice. By then SLP had been voted into power, so the task of dealing with yet another consequence of a dysfunctional UWP government fell to Dr. Kenny Anthony's administration.

Faced with such American angst, the prime minister, Dr. Kenny Anthony, secured the services of CARICOM's Implementation Agency for Crime and Security (IMPACS) to conduct an investigation into the killings. The resulting IMPACS report, which concluded that the police officers involved in the killings "must be prosecuted," was shared with both the US government and the St. Lucia Director of Public Prosecution (DPP). In so doing the prime minister was accused of bungling the process, kowtowing to the US, compromising St. Lucia's sovereignty, demoralizing the police force, and undermining the integrity and independence of the DPP, the official body for investigating and ruling on such alleged crimes.[15,16,17]

Rick Wayne, Kenny Anthony's longtime nemesis, well known for his ability to influence the results of elections and hence the accolade "Prime Minister Maker," night after night, got on his talk show screaming IMPACS, and how this was the biggest problem facing the country, and how dare Kenny Anthony take this course of action. Listening to Rick Wayne, and without the benefit of any other information, one could hardly be blamed for believing the extra-judicial killings had taken place under Kenny Anthony's administration, or worse he was the one who had ordered the killings or had pulled the triggers. Therefore, it may not surprise anyone if Rick Wayne's nightly tirade on IMPACS had single-handedly caused some uninformed citizens to vote against Kenny Anthony's SLP and in favor of Chastanet's UWP in the 2016 general elections. Clearly, Kenny Anthony has paid a heavy price for expelling Rick Wayne from the Senate during his first term as prime minister (1997-2001).

There was the St. Jude debacle. On the evening of September 9, 2009, a fire razed St. Jude Hospital in the town of Vieux Fort, causing 5 deaths, destroying the operating theaters and the surgical and pediatric wards, and exposing asbestos insulations. In the aftermath of the fire, the Stephenson King UWP government had few options but to relocate the hospital to the nearby George Odlum Stadium.

The next general elections (2011) was two years away, so no one was surprised when the government erected a large billboard at the entrance of Vieux Fort boldly announcing the rehabilitation of the hospital by 2011. Elections came but the hospital was nowhere near completion. UWP lost the elections to the Kenny Anthony Labour Party. Four years and EC$118 million later, with another general elections (2016) around the corner, the hospital was still incomplete, and no one had a clue of when it would leave the George Odlum Stadium, its adopted home, and return to its original home.

Ironically, the SLP which had criticized the UWP government for failing to complete the hospital in two years, failed to do so in four years even though they had had a head start. The fiasco, travesty, even, that the rebuilding of St. Jude Hospital turned out to be was amply captured in Untold Stories.[18]

Meantime, things went from bad to worse. Millions of dollars of donated equipment rusted to uselessness in storage awaiting the completion of the hospital. The Chinese-built and donated George Odlum Stadium never envisioned housing a hospital, thus in its new home St. Jude was at best a make-shift, disaster relief hospital. Worse, the stadium, which was in a deep state of deterioration, needed almost as much of a restoration rescue as the burnt-up St. Jude. For example, the stadium's roof was raining fiberglass fibers. Unsurprising, upon official inspection the make-shift hospital was deemed grossly deficient, inhospitable, and an occupational safety and health hazard. So much so, that one doctor described the conditions as a "dungeon of shame."[19]

The public consensus was that the adverse conditions at the makeshift hospital were causing needless deaths. A St. Lucian living in New York revealed with great anger that he could overlook the government's shortcomings in education, road infrastructure, job creation, etc., but he could never forgive the government for not completing the hospital, for playing political football with the lives of people, for what is more important than people's health? Clearly, the Kenny Anthony SLP government had underestimated how much importance the populace placed on a viable and fully functioning St. Jude Hospital. With elections looming and the hospital still far from completion, Chastanet and his UWP government would do well to take heed.

There was the unease that Kenny Anthony took too long to implement projects. Case in point, the Hewanorra Airport Redevelopment Project. Since 2014 the government with the help of the International Finance Corporation (IFC) of the World Bank, had undertaken to privatize the operations of Hewanorra International Airport (HIA) in an arrangement called Public Private Partnership (PPP), whereby a private entity would assume the responsibility of redeveloping, operating, and maintaining the airport, while the St. Lucia Air and Sea Ports Authority (SLASPA), the custodian of the airport, would be relegated to the role of regulating the operator. Under this arrangement, government would collect corporate profit taxes and SLASPA would receive a share of corporate proceeds. In May 2015 it was announced that the private partner contract would be awarded in October 2015, but no such contract was awarded. Then it was announced that the contract would be awarded in January 2016. January came and went but no contracts were awarded, and then there was silence, and soon thereafter (May 19, 2016) instead of the HIA Redevelopment Project contract announcement, the prime minister announced that general elections would be held on June 6, 2016.

Clearly, when the impression that Dr. Kenny Anthony was too indecisive and actionless was juxtaposed against a vigorous and seemingly confident Allen Chastanet running his election campaign on the notion that as a businessman he knows how to get things done and in good time, and that he would run the country as a business, Allen Chastanet was looking increasingly appealing.

And then there was the Juffali affair.[20] In November 2012, 57-year-old Saudi billionaire, Dr. Sheikh Walid Juffali, married 25-year-old Lebanese model and TV presenter, Loujain Adada, while still married to American former Pirelli Calendar model, Christina Estrada. The marriage was quite kosher with Dr. Juffali's Islamic religion, which permits multiple wives (up to four), but not so with his second wife, Christina Estrada, who found out about the wedding after the fact. The former Pirelli Calendar model promptly started divorce proceedings, and the couple was officially divorced two years later, in 2014. But there was the issue of the divorce settlement claim. Apparently, taking advantage of a seemingly more sympathetic court and having an eye on Dr. Juffali's UK real estate valued at an estimated £140 million, Estrada filed her divorce settlement claim of £196 million in UK courts that she argued was necessary to meet her "reasonable needs" following her estrangement from her husband. Notwithstanding Estrada's needs, if allowed the claim would make history as the UK's largest settlement award.

It seems the Chess game had just begun.

In April 2014, Dr. Juffali secured an appointment as St. Lucia's permanent representative to the London based International Maritime Organization (IMO), thereby gaining diplomatic immunity in the UK, and halting the divoice settlement proceedings. Allen Chastanet, the UWP, the St. Lucian public, and the world, even, paid attention when, in response to the news of Dr. Juffali's IMO St. Lucia appointment, both the British Foreign Office and Estrada's lawyers urged the St. Lucian government to relieve Dr. Juffali of his diplomatic immunity (which they suspected he was using to keep his ex-wife away from his wealth), so that the courts could compel him to testify in his divorce settlement proceedings.

In response, on November 11, 2015, the government of St. Lucia issued a press release[21] that one suspects was penned by the then St. Lucia UK High Commissioner, Dr. Ernest Hilaire. The press release said that Dr. Juffali was an outstanding corporate and world citizen with many prestigious awards to prove it. That he and his family had a tradition of serving as diplomats of other countries, and besides serving on the IMO, Dr. Juffali was helping to promote St. Lucia and draw foreign investments to the country. As further proof of Dr. Juffali's value to St. Lucia, the press release indicated that he was helping to establish in St. Lucia a medical research industry and a much needed Global Diabetes Research Centre given St. Lucia's and the rest of the Caribbean's epidemic prevalence of diabetes. The press release then explained that not only is a divorce proceeding a private matter that the government should not get involved in but complying with the request of the British Foreign Office and Estrada's lawyers would set an undesirable precedent that would undermine St. Lucia's diplomatic integrity world-wide.

Notwithstanding the press release, if Dr. Juffali's ex-wife's accusation that he never attended an IMO meeting is true, then Juffali may have benefited St. Lucia and the SLP administration in other ways but not with regard to the IMO.

Unsurprisingly, with so much at stake, the former super model did not buy it; neither did Chastanet and the UWP; and neither did Rick Wayne. In fact, in addition to IMPACS, Rick Wayne now had another bone to chew on and another blow to strike at Kenny Anthony on his weekly talk show. Listening to Rick Wayne, one got the impression that from IMPACS to VAT (and other taxes) to Juffali to construction tax (and customs duties) exemptions for perceived cronies, the Kenny Anthony SLP administration could do no right.

The courts waded in. In February 2016, pronouncing Juffali's claim of legal immunity as "spurious", the High Court dismissed the claim. Juffali's team appealed the ruling. The Court of Appeal upheld Juffali's claim of diplomatic immunity, but, regarding his immunity as irrelevant to the divorce claim, allowed the court proceedings to advance.

Meantime, back in St. Lucia, on May 19, 2016, the prime minister, Dr. Kenny D. Anthony, surprised most St. Lucians when he announced general elections for June 6, 2016. Elections were not required by law until April 2017, but the prime minister felt compelled to advance the date to, as he said, secure "peace, stability and certainty."[22] Of course, one wonders whether the premature call to elections was to take advantage of the turmoil in the UWP camp and/or the administration had a full slate of programs and projects to implement and therefore wanted the certainty of five more years in office before fully showing its hand. Nonetheless, amidst outcry of the unfairness of Dr. Anthony's early and unexpected election call, the country entered into full election mode; yellow and red crowding out all other colors, the UWP slogan, *Yo Pè*, They Afraid, ringing across the country.

However, it seemed that, in terms of the elections, Dr. Kenny Anthony had more to worry about than just Chastanet, the UWP, and St. Lucian voters. For according to rumors, Christina Estrada took time off her high-profile divorce claim proceedings and came to St. Lucia where she stayed at Coconut Bay Resort, in Vieux Fort, the prime minister's electoral district. But she did not come empty handed. Rumors had it she came with bags full of money ostensibly to provide incentives for St. Lucians, Vieux Fortians especially, to vote against Kenny Anthony and his Labour Party. Apparently, the former super model wanted not only to put the SLP out of power but to ensure Kenny Anthony lost his seat.

On June 6, 2016, Estrada tasted sweet victory when the supposedly beleaguered Chastanet-led UWP ousted the overconfident Kenny Anthony SLP out of power with an 11-6 majority. She would taste even sweeter victory, when in July 2016, shortly before Juffali died of cancer, she was awarded a divorce claim settlement of £75 million, making it the largest such award in UK history and £35 million more than Juffali's first wife, Basma Al-Sulaiman, had received in her 2000 divorce settlement.

And so it came to pass that Allen Chastanet became prime minister of St. Lucia despite being considered a political novice, undistinguished in terms of intellect and accomplishments, seemingly lacking the capacity for the job, a non-St. Lucian born of the politically incorrect race, culturally speaking barely St. Lucian, and heading a political party in disarray.

Part III

The Problem with Allen Chastanet

Dame Calliopa Pearlette Louisy GCSL, GCMG
(born 8 June 1946)

Longest serving governor general of St. Lucia (1997 -
2017). Raised the cultural profile of St. Lucia. Brought
greater civility to the political process, and by example
helped foster a more civil and humane society.

7

IT'S ALL ABOUT CULTURE

In June 2016, the UWP came to power following a surprise defeat of the incumbent SLP by 11 to 6 electoral seats. After Labour supporters had gotten over their disappointment of losing the elections and after some St. Lucians, especially those who have been exposed to North American and European racism, had overcome their shock, shame, even, of a white man presiding over their predominantly black country, they had probably consoled themselves with: *Well, this may be a blessing in disguise, for it's not like the Kenny Anthony-led Labour government had set the world on fire; and Allen Chastanet, a wealthy, bonafide businessman, owner and manager of award-winning twin hotels, had run his campaign on the premise that he would manage the country as a business, and he would roll up his sleeves and get to work creating jobs and unleashing economic progress. So maybe, just maybe, Chastanet will be the hero able to go where Dr. Kenny Anthony with all his academic and intellectual prowess and rarified regional stature could not go, and bring home the elixir of national prosperity.*

Apparently, even Allen Chastanet may have seen himself as the hero who would restore the UWP and St. Lucia to the glory days of John Compton. When his father had discouraged him from accepting Compton's call to serve as tourism minister and instead focus on his plans to start his own business, Allen said, "Dad, when a prime minister calls you to serve your country you do not refuse unless there are grave health issues stopping you from accepting his offer." And that he could make a much bigger contribution to St. Lucia as minister of tourism than as manager of his father's 100 room hotels. Later, witnessing the demise of John Compton and the subsequent fall of the UWP government into a dysfunctional state, Michael Chastanet had pleaded with his son to resign from government, but Allen Chastanet refused because he reasoned to do so would be to dishonor the memory of John Compton and would set back the country's tourism industry.

Yet four years later, one is made to understand, especially by Labour supporters, that Allen Chastanet is no hero. Many voices of anguish are castigating him as a villain who has to go. The reasons for this cry of anguish and castigation of Allen Chastanet as a villain have been well articulated. However, despite the multiplicity of voices decrying the UWP administration's handling of the country and pointing out how it has undermined the nation and its citizens, some St. Lucians, especially UWP supporters, remain unconvinced of Chastanet's villainy and that an SLP administration would be any better.

Whether an SLP administration would do better in terms of economic expansion, job creation, and employment, and in terms of crime reduction and other social and health indicators may be debatable, but what seems clear is that there has never been a previous administration that is perceived as being so much against the best interest of the country.

Therefore, despite the many voices that have weighed in on the subject, it may be useful to once again clarify, investigate why the Chastanet-led UWP government is viewed in such bad light, forcing some St. Lucians, SLP stalwarts in particular, to pronounce it the worst government in St. Lucia's history. Some even saying that if Chastanet's party were to win a second term, there may not even be a country left worth fighting for. Such serious accusations require investigation to determine, if nothing else, the extent to which the Chastanet administration has outdone its predecessors in terms of villainy—lacking integrity, violation of public trust, incompetency, and not putting the interest of the country first.

To begin with, the prime minister is perceived as being disrespectful and insensitive to the people. For example, he was accused of referring to St. Lucians as "barking dogs", "mendicants", and "jackasses", and of marching in a UWP march alongside a placard that said "NICE: Niggas In Charge of Employment."[1]

The prime minister was also accused of pronouncing "... economics has no conscience ... colonialism had a conscience... "[2] It is not clear what the prime minister had in mind when he made the statement, whether he was on a roll and was simply reeling out what sounded good to his ears, or whether he was simply emphasizing that economics, at least laissez-faire economics, was impersonal, was no respecter of persons, by contrasting it with colonialism. However his rationale, "colonialism has a conscience," is not far removed from "slavery had a conscience," which clearly would be objectionable to descendants of those who were enslaved.

Such insensitivity is particularly jarring given the country's recent history of slavery (less than three generations removed from slavery) and colonialism and now globalization (which, for small nations like St. Lucia, is another name for imperialism) and that the prime minister who is considered white or almost white is presiding over a country whose population is overwhelmingly black and descendants of African slaves.

Jarring also because of the *Black Lives Matter* movement and the recent spike in America of white police violence on Blacks. Of course, the prime minister, in the heat of the moment, may have been firing shots at SLP stalwarts and party hacks, and it may not have been his intention to disrespect and disparage the population. And it is not like the opposition has been holding back punches. As noted previously, they have accused him of being a conman, an empty head, a "massa", and of lying about having college degrees. However, part of what makes one fit for high office is the knack of knowing what to say, how to say, and when to say. After all, the wrong word spoken at the wrong time can lead to wars.

The prime minister has been accused, culturally speaking, of being a non-St. Lucian. Meaning he is not steeped in, or he is not *okouwan* with St. Lucian culture. If so, herein may lie an explanation for the prime minister's inadvertent insensitivity to the population, meaning he just does not get it, or he just cannot get it right.

Indeed, in Chapter 4 evidence was presented that suggested there is a basis for the accusation that culturally Allen Chastanet is barely a St. Lucian.

In this regard, the prime minister stands alone. John Compton, whose people were seafaring and came from St. Vincent, was accused of being a non-St. Lucian born, but he was never accused of being out of step with St. Lucian culture. For who could be regarded more St. Lucian than a Kwéyòl speaking John Compton with an understated personality, a banana farmer driving to his farm on a rickety van often with pickup riders at the back, equipped with a razor-blade sharp cutlass and dressed in rubber boots and banana stained clothes.

In a 2004 interview with Jacintha Annius-Lee,[3] Compton said, "I did not know I was not a St. Lucian until I entered politics. I always accepted myself as St. Lucian." In sharp contrast, One may not be surprised if Chastanet's detractors insist that he only discovered he is a St. Lucian when he wanted to enter politics. For before he stepped on the political stage, most St. Lucians were not aware of his existence. Moreover, he has said that he is a product of Canada.

In Chapter 6 it was mentioned that Allen Chastanet and some other St. Lucians have labeled Kenny Anthony a "massa," implying his ancestors were slave masters. However, unlike Allen Chastanet, the St. Lucian-ness of Kenny Anthony, who was raised by his single St. Lucian mother and who did most of his schooling in St. Lucia and the West Indies, has never been questioned. This suggests that sometimes it is not one's skin tone that matters or the sins of one's ancestors or even where one is originally from but the extent to which one has become an integral part of the society and developed an affinity with the people and the culture.

To further emphasize that culture matters, consider Samuel P. Huntington's path-breaking book, *The Clash of Civilizations and the Remaking of World Order*,[4] in which he defines a civilization as the "highest cultural grouping of people and the broadest level of cultural identity people have short of that which distinguishes humans from other species." Based on this definition, he classifies the Anglophone Caribbean as a civilization unto itself. Thus, culturally speaking, someone born and raised in St. Vincent is likely to consider herself a Vincentian, and then a West Indian. Higher up, the next closest groupings would be the Western, African, or Latin American civilizations. However, grouping herself under anyone of these civilizations requires a stretch, because the cultural gap between the West Indies and these other groupings is sufficiently large to make our Vincentian hesitant to classify herself as belonging to them. Therefore, the highest cultural grouping with which she can comfortably identify is the West Indies, hence the West Indies could be considered a separate civilization.

Huntington also points out that because members of the same civilization share the same basic core values and beliefs (culture by another name) there is a greater level of trust, comfort, and ease of understanding and communication among them. Therefore, members of the same civilization tend to trade and engage in greater economic and other exchanges with each other, and efforts at forming economic, political, sporting and cultural unions tend to be more successful than those that involve peoples of different civilizations (different cultural groupings).

Another facet of this concept of civilization that bears out is that members of the same civilization (another name for cultural grouping) tend to be more empathetic to each other and more willing to help each other in times of crisis than someone of a different civilization facing a similar situation. So this partly explains why, say the US, might be quicker to come to the aid of an European country than an African country; why the Anglophone Caribbean might feel more compelled to help say Grenada than Haiti, which Huntington classifies as a civilization unto itself.

So the extent to which Chastanet sees himself as Canadian or European as opposed to St. Lucian or West Indian is the extent to which he may have greater empathy for persons from these parts, and when there is a conflict between the interest of St. Lucians and that of these foreign entities, he may be confused regarding whose interest he, as prime minister of St. Lucia, should give priority to. In other words, he may be confused as to which side he is on.

The prime minister of Barbados, Mia Mottley, has also stressed the significance of culture to a society.[5] She sees culture as playing a central role in the progress of the region. She reasoned that many current regional problems, including political unrest, gun violence, and the bleaching of skins, stem from issues of identity and cultural confidence; and that the lack of cultural confidence or self-contempt by another name (feeling lesser than other people) — which emanates from smallness, history of subjugation, and dearth of economic, military, and technological prominence — partly explains the region's underdevelopment.

The first person who came to mind when she mentioned self-contempt and the lack of cultural confidence was Trinidad's Nobel Laureate, V.S. Naipaul, who, apparently equating production and meaningfulness with such things as airplanes, automobiles, machinery, etc., while neglecting cultural products, wrote: "History is built around achievement and creation; and nothing was created in the West Indies."[6] Naipaul's statement may be regarded as the epitome of self-contempt, and the West Indies' disproportionate cultural and intellectual output, personified by the likes of Walcott, Naipaul himself, Bob Marley, and many others, belies his pronouncement.

The second person who came to mind was Allen Chastanet. Because, like Naipaul, does he present another example of the self-contempt that Mia Mottley speaks so eloquently about? Is he seeing St. Lucia and St. Lucians as lesser because they do not have skyscrapers, bullet trains, and billionaires, hence his desire to turn the island into a Miami Beach or Dubai Palm Island replica? Is it this self-contempt that many sense that has made the prime minister so abhorrent to them?

8

PUTTING FOREIGNERS FIRST

The second accusation of Chastanet is that he is intent on siphoning resources from the population for the benefit of foreign and private entities. So it may be fruitful to examine the events/projects/initiatives that have given rise to this charge.

Desert Star Holdings (DSH)

August 2016, barely two months after winning the general elections, Prime Minister Allen Chastanet signed an agreement[1] with Desert Star Holdings (DSH), a Hong Kong-based equine management and investment company (led by Teo Ah Khing,[2] a billionaire Malaysian native with Chinese roots) for a development project expected to transform over 800 acres of Vieux Fort lands into what is called the Pearl of the Caribbean[3] that promises a marina, horse racecourse, resort hotels, luxury villas and apartments, a shopping mall complex, a casino, and originally a boardwalk and museum in Vieux Fort's Mankótè Mangrove Forest, the island's largest stand of mangroves. The Pearl of the Caribbean was first touted as a US$1 billion investment, and then a US$2.6 billion investment, and finally a US$3.0 billion investment. Regardless, if implemented, the initiative would be tantamount to depositing overnight an entire city on Vieux Fort's seaboard and turning the area into a replica Miami Beach and Dubai Palm Island, all in one.

However, it turned out that the devil was in the details, or in the signed agreements (which were leaked to the public), or between the lines. According to the signed agreements, some of these lands will be sold to the developer at US$60,000 to US$90,000 per acre, or US$1.4 to US$2.1 per square foot, considerably less than current market rates, which starts at about US$5.5 (EC$15). Other lands will be leased at US$1 per acre per year for 99 years. Where the asking price of private lands exceeds US$90,000 per acre, the government will pay the amount over the US$90,000. For some lands, the developer will have the option of leasing or buying; and if buying, the developer will only pay for a parcel of land after the development for which the parcel was earmarked is completed. The developer will be free to sell any such lands acquired from government to other investors at whatever price and terms he decides. Notwithstanding, if after two years of the project launch the developer has not secured at least 200 investors for the project, upon the developer's request the government is obligated to not only buy back the land but pay the developer the full value of infrastructure established on the land.

The government will pay for removing and relocating any structure or infrastructure or public utility in the way of the development, and will be responsible for bringing public utilities such as water, electricity, sewage, refuse collection, postal service, and telecommunications to the doorsteps of the development. The government is also responsible for establishing an Educational Training Fund for the equine industry, and an Equine Disease-Free Zone to safeguard the health of the imported thoroughbreds, and those to be exported. The developer will be exempt from income tax on interest earned, value-added tax, property tax, alien landholding license fees, stamp duty and vendors tax, customs duties on imports and on alternative energy, corporate tax, withholding tax, and any other tax exemptions allowed under the Incentives Act & Tourism Stimulus and Investment Act. In addition, the government cannot approve any new licenses for casinos, horse racing wagering and betting, and free trade zones for any other development in any part of the country.

On top of all this, most of the DSH project (or at least its initial phases) will be financed not by the developer but by proceeds from the sale of St. Lucian passports. The only capitalization pledge made by the developer in the agreement is US$5 million earmarked for Phase 1 of the development, involving the establishment of the horse racetrack and related activities. But it would appear the pledge of US$5 million was not fulfilled, and most monies spent so far on the project are believed to have come from the government.

DSH will be directly responsible for the selling of the citizenships, which can be an indefinite number, the proceeds of which will be placed in an offshore escrow account from which DSH will withdraw at its discretion; its only accountability to government is that it provides notice of each withdrawal. Any monies left in the escrow account at the completion of the project will go to the developer. Moreover, to expressly cover marketing and agent cost the developer will be rewarded upwards of US$15,000 for every concluded investment (sale of citizenship).

Now, one would think, after agreeing to give away so much that the government would gain or be rewarded with shares or equity in the development, but the agreements make no mention of such. Neither is there any provision for local investors to acquire shares or equity.

So then, what is in this deal for St. Lucia? Well, here is what the agreement states, "it is understood that the government has agreed to the foregoing on the understanding and expectation that the approved project is intended to develop the land significantly and to lead to significant job creation and retention and shall be construed as a fundamental term of this agreement."

The statement suggests that the government is not even sure what is in it for St. Lucia. The jobs created will go to whom: St. Lucians, Chinese? It is difficult to say, because the agreements spell out that the developer is free to source its workers from anywhere it chooses, local or foreign, without interference from government. The land development is to whose benefit? It is not for the use of St. Lucians. It is not even clear that St. Lucians will be allowed to access it.

Moreover, no limit was placed on the sale of passports, the sale of citizenship. Consider the overnight impact of say 20 to 50 thousand Chinese nationals acquiring St. Lucian citizenship on the country's political process, on its election results, not to mention the extent to which this mass entry would change the very character of the country (a country of only 170 thousand people), its sociological and demographic landscape. It seems a gross insensitivity, a gross oversight, to have ignored this possible phenomenon.

Therefore, based on the DSH agreement, Vieux Fortians, SLP supporters, and other informed St. Lucians can hardly be faulted for concluding that the government is intent on taking away their resources and handing them over to foreign entities, and that the government is more about serving foreign interest than local interest. And what is most perplexing to many Vieux Fortians is that one would think that when foreign developers, especially billionaires, come to one's country, they would arrive with a feeling of generosity, bearing gifts, even; yet this arrangement was anything but generous to St. Lucians. On the contrary, it would appear that the country was paying the developer to siphon away its resources.

Now, UWP sympathizers may retort with: *Dr. Kenny Anthony would have likely signed this same agreement had his party held on to power in 2016, because, after all, Allen Chastanet found the DSH proposal on the table, ready for signing, when he came to power.* And there may be some truth to that. The former prime minister has admitted that his administration had been in discussions with the DSH developer for 18 months and the reason it had taken so long was that the government had been negotiating a better deal for St. Lucia than what was reflected in the agreement Chastanet signed. So much so, that the former prime minister said that the agreement the prime minister signed had been the starting point of the negotiations, but by the 2016 elections the government had made considerable progress toward a more advantageous arrangement for St. Lucia. The former prime minister had also expressed concerns about the loss of sovereignty implied in allowing a foreign entity to administer the country's passport sales, and that Vieux Fort horsemen, chiefly responsible for keeping alive the tradition of horseracing in St. Lucia, would be left out of the equation.

One will never know what final agreement the SLP administration would have signed, but the fact that it wrestled so long with the negotiations such that elections came and it still could not announce the project (when this would have been a feather in its cap), suggests that the government may have placed the best interest of the country above the expediency of winning a general election. After 18 months the former administration could not bring itself to sign an agreement with DSH, yet it took Allen Chastanet just two months to sign that same agreement, which turned out to be atrocious, detrimental to the interest of Vieux Fort and St. Lucia.

OJO Labs

In 2017 the government enticed OJO Labs,[4,5] a Texas-based enterprise billed as an artificial intelligence (AI) company, to open a branch at the Hewanorra Free-zone Complex in Vieux Fort. The company explained that the core of its business is the "building of an automated intelligence assistant for the real estate industry," regarded as the "first of its kind," which is "basically technology and neural networks that can automatically respond to consumers' questions and inquiries." When fully operational the company is expected to employ upwards of 700 full-time employees.

Some critics have described the Vieux Fort OJO Labs establishment not as the "state-of-the-art" AI contact center it is christened, but as a low-paying glorified call center. However, in a country that faces perennial unemployment rates of 15 to 24 percent, and youth unemployment of over 30 percent, 700 hundred jobs is nothing to smirk at, more so since even though these jobs are not as high-paying as one would like, their pay and working conditions are arguably better than that of store and gas station attendants.

Moreover, although one cannot vouch for the high-techness of OJO Labs, and although one is not sure that Chastanet's administration has articulated a vision for Vieux Fort of transforming the area into a Silicon-Valley-like high-tech zone, OJO Labs can well be the start of the fulfillment of such a reality. After all, as often repeated, *realizing most endeavors is more a matter of will and desire than a matter of resources.* A Vieux Fort Silicon Valley replica only requires a plan of action involving infrastructure, proactively enticing foreign hi-tech companies, fostering homegrown companies and sending St. Lucians by the hundreds to obtain IT training and degrees.

Imagine that. In 2019, about 2,910 or 32.4 percent of Vieux Fort's labor force of 8983 workers was unemployed.[6] Therefore, all what was required to reduce the district's unemployment rate to zero (assuming all the jobs went to workers from the district) were roughly four OJO Labs.

So far, so good. However, what troubles many St. Lucians is that not only has the government reportedly extended considerable concessions to OJO Labs and has borne the cost of providing and retrofitting the company's place of operation, but it reportedly paid OJO Labs' wages and operating expenses for an undisclosed period.[7] Yet the government has provided no indication of the full dollar amount of its contributions to the company, nor what percentage of ownership it will gain for its input, and whether there will be any kind of profit sharing.

Once again, like with DSH, Allen Chastanet may have placed St. Lucia, a Third World, resource-starved country, in the ironic position of subsidizing rich foreign entities from rich countries when logic would have suggested the reverse.

How does this compare with previous administrations? Well, it is no secret that St. Lucian and other Caribbean governments have been extending generous concessions and leasing lands at zero cost as a means of enticing Foreign Direct Investments (FDI). And one may not doubt that previous St. Lucian governments would have considered paying the wages of an established company as a short-term stopgap to prevent them from going under. But one suspects that, unless the government is gaining shares in the enterprise, its payment of the wages and operating expenses of a start-up company is unprecedented. Such an arrangement suggests either desperation by the government to create employment or personal gains to government officials and their associates or both.

Another thought. If OJO Labs is part of a plan to develop Vieux Fort into a high-tech nerve center, could not the government use CIP funds to form direct partnerships with such firms to entice them to St. Lucia? One suspects that St. Lucians do not have a problem with forming such partnerships; they have a problem with the country getting nothing in return.

Cabot Saint Lucia

Destined for Point Hardy, a 375-acre peninsula at the northern end of the island with 1.5 miles of coastline, Cabot Saint Lucia[8] promises a luxury resort with a 50-suite boutique hotel, three restaurants, boutique retail shops, Cabot Spa and clubhouse, an 18-hole golf course, and villas with price tags ranging from $760,000 to $10 million.

Besides its employment opportunities and synergies with other sectors of the economy, the development is expected to improve the island's marketability and enhance its reputation as a high-end visitors' destination. Apart from possible environmental degradation and the limiting of access to the Queen's Chain, few St. Lucians would have a quarrel with the development. Who is against employment and economic upliftment?

However, as with DSH and OJO Labs, St. Lucians have a problem with their country financing yet another project by a rich entity from a rich country. The St. Lucia National Insurance Corporation (NIC), which encompasses workers' pension fund, medical insurance, and unemployment compensation, through the urging of the prime minister, is financing Cabot Saint Lucia with a loan of EC$30 million.[9] Considering that part of the developer's game plan is to raise capital by pre-selling lots to prospective homeowners (luxury flats/villas), the NIC loan is likely to represent a significant portion of the developer's upfront financial capital. So although Mike Keiser, a world-renowned golf resort owner and developer and one principal of Cabot Saint Lucia, is touted as a billionaire, his St. Lucia golf resort might be built largely with *other people's money*, including that of poor, hard-working St. Lucians.

Now, the NIC's bylaws[10] allows it to grow the fund by judicious investments. So in making a loan to Cabot Saint Lucia, the NIC was operating within its mandate. Notwithstanding, the transaction raises some concerns. Why a premier golf course resort developer like Cabot could not secure finance from mainstream financial institutions such as commercial banks in its home country or even in St. Lucia? Is it because these mainstream institutions have access to information the NIC is not privy to, or, given pressure from the prime minister, the NIC, whose board of directors would have been appointed by the government, was not at liberty to deny Cabot the loan?

This is a pertinent concern, for according to Caribbean News Global,[11] companies heavily dependent on government funding and concessions make for bad investments and loans and do not represent a model of development or success. Yet by its very nature the NIC should be investing in low risk, high return ventures.

In responding to concerns raised by the opposition political party, the NIC said the loan is 100 percent secured. But secured by whom, the government? And with what?

Therefore, who could blame Dr. Ernest Hilaire,[9] SLP deputy party leader, when he asked:

> Why do we need to use our pension funds to finance the purchase of lands for a billionaire? What is the security (assets/equity) against which NIC investment/loan was made? Is it true that the investor had been trying to buy this property for over three years and could not close on the property purchase? Does the investor love our NIC so much that the NIC was searched out to present such a sweetheart deal?

9

PUTTING ST. LUCIANS LAST

Many St. Lucians, SLP supporters especially, may confess that what makes the notion that the prime minister is serving the interest of foreign entities at the expense of citizens even more vexing is that while he seems hell-bent on facilitating rich, foreign entities, he appears to go out of his way to dismantle programs geared toward helping the most disadvantaged of St. Lucians and programs that speak to nation-building, sovereignty, and patrimony. This constitutes the third accusation of the Chastanet government; that in the eyes of Allen Chastanet St. Lucians do not matter. If so, what programs/institutions have the government dismantled or discontinued that have so irked St. Lucians?

The Distress Support Fund

The Distress Support Fund, established by the former SLP government to provide assistance to victims of fire, hurricanes, and other disasters, was one of the casualties of the Allen Chastanet UWP government. Yet in a country where about a quarter of the population and one-third of children live in poverty,[1] where there are few safety nets, and where many people cannot afford property insurance, the Distress Support Fund was no luxury.

It is not clear whether Chastanet's policy was that such a fund was best financed by charitable donations, but, in 2019, after witnessing two separate fires in the Castries area that destroyed nine homes, former CARICOM economist and St. Lucian diplomat, Peter Lansiquot, was so convinced of the necessity of the Distress Support Fund, that he took it upon himself to establish a replacement fund, the People's Distress Fund,[2] to be funded by donations from St. Lucians at home and abroad.

The St. Lucia Jazz Festival

The St. Lucia Jazz Festival, later renamed the St. Lucia Jazz & Arts Festival, was first held in 1992 to extend the tourist season into May. By the time Allen Chastanet became prime minister in 2016, the festival had celebrated its 25th anniversary and was ranked among the top three best music festivals in the Caribbean.[3] It would be no exaggeration to say that the jazz festival had helped place St. Lucia on the world map, and had become a grand and glorious affair, a source of pride to many St. Lucians. The St. Lucia Jazz Festival was one thing St. Lucia had gotten right. It matched and even exceeded international standards.

Notwithstanding, for many St. Lucians the great beauty of the St. Lucia Jazz & Arts Festival was its democratic disposition. Jazz shows, both free and paid, were held throughout the island, allowing vendors and service providers in different communities to share in the spoils, and making it possible for the youngest and/or the poorest of St. Lucians to enjoy world-class music concerts. Imagine the horizon-expanding impact on a child witnessing right in her community the best the world has to offer.

It seems this was too good to be true. Because to the dismay of many St. Lucians, the Chastanet administration seemingly turned the festival into an elitist affair by limiting it to the north of the island in the vicinity of its tourism mecca and keeping most of the events at one venue, the Royalton Saint Lucia Resort and Spa. Following the change, Jazz, an event St. Lucians used to look forward to with great anticipation would come and go and people would not even notice. Weeks after the event has passed, people would ask: "When is Jazz?" The festival became yet another depiction of the notion that, in the eyes of the prime minister, the best of what St. Lucia has to offer is for tourists and not for locals, which contrasts with the Kenny Anthony administration, under whose domain the St. Lucia Jazz Festival was expanded to include literature, theatre, dance, and visual arts events (hence the name change to Saint Lucia Jazz & Arts Festival) to ensure that St. Lucians benefit maximally from the festival.

The National Trust

In his great wisdom, recognizing the inevitable conflict between development imperatives and heritage conservation, Sir John Compton established the St. Lucia National Trust in 1975 as an independent statutory body with a mandate to preserve and protect the country's patrimony, i.e., its natural and cultural heritage. The Trust manages such protected areas as national landmarks, historical sites, environmental protection areas, and nature reserves.

The Chastanet administration rolled back 42 years of history when in 2017 it removed the EC$700,000 annual subvention of the National Trust, which represented about 20 percent of the Trust's budget. The prime minister cited the need to remedy the country's cash flow problems as the reason for the removal of the subvention. However, the move followed on the heels of the Trust's objection to certain aspects of the DSH development and to a government-sanctioned dolphinarium (a longtime dream of Michael Chastanet, the prime minister's father) at Pigeon Island

National Park in the north of the island. Therefore, many viewed the government's decision as victimization — retaliation against the Trust for opposing government initiatives.[4,5]

The Walcott House

Derek Walcott, winner of the 1992 literature Nobel Prize, is perhaps St. Lucia's most celebrated son of the soil. Each year the island hosts a month-long Nobel Laureate Festival in commemoration of its two Nobel Laureates — Sir Derek Walcott, and Sir Arthur Lewis who won the 1979 Nobel Prize for economics. Derek Walcott, along with his twin brother, Roderick Walcott, helped establish the 1950s St. Lucia Arts Guild that led the way in West Indian theatre and that sparked a St. Lucia cultural renaissance.[6]

It was therefore fitting when, under the auspices of the National Trust and funding from the Taiwanese government, the house where the Walcott brothers were raised was transformed into a museum, the Walcott House, thereby helping to preserve a significant aspect of the country's cultural heritage. The National Trust is responsible for the upkeep and running of the museum which has an operating cost of about EC$80,000 per year. With the removal of its subvention, the Trust was forced to close the Walcott House.[7] Some suspect that the closing of the Walcott House was another facet of government victimization, i.e., retaliation against the artist community for vehemently opposing a government plan to relocate the National Cultural Center and the Cultural Development Foundation from their current location on Barnard Hill, overlooking the Castries waterfront, to make way for a temporary courthouse.

According to the Trust,[8] the Walcott House was only the first stage of a EC$16 million Walcott Place & Grass Street Urban Enhancement Project toward which the Taiwanese government had provided a grant of EC$7.5 million. The House costs only a fraction of the EC$7.5 million of the Taiwanese donation. Thus, as the House is closed and the balance of the project is in limbo, what has happened (or what does the government intend to do) with the balance of the Taiwanese endowment is anyone's guess. Isn't it ironic that the Walcott House is closed because of lack of funds, yet millions of dollars contributed partly for its establishment are sitting idle or worse may have been diverted to unsanctioned uses?

To provide an indication of the significance of Walcott, and hence the Walcott House, to the artist community (local and international), consider the reaction of Jamaica Kincaid, an internationally acclaimed author with Antiguan roots, at her presentation of the 2017 Derek Walcott Lecture, a highlight of the St. Lucia Nobel Laureate Festival. She was appalled of the upkeep of the Derek Walcott House. She said that although she is not from St. Lucia, Derek Walcott has meant a lot to her as a writer and a Caribbean person. "He and his writing are repositories of the Caribbean journey."[9] She said that the upkeep of the House was a disgrace to the honor of the Nobel Laureate, and she would be willing to contribute to the maintenance of the House if that is what it will take. It was a shameful moment for the St. Lucia artist community.

Radio St. Lucia

The state sponsored Radio St. Lucia (RSL) was another program/activity that met the axe of the Allen Chastanet government. In justifying the closure of the radio station, the prime minister explained that despite a government subvention of EC$410,000, the station was riddled with debt. Moreover, unlike when the station was first established, there are now many outlets for information dissemination, including cell phones, social media, several television stations, and a multitude of radio stations.[10]

Notwithstanding, RSL was regarded as a public radio station. It served as a community news bulletin board. Its music playlist contained a much larger percentage of local content than that of other radio stations, and it carried cultural programs that set it apart. It was a repository of St. Lucian culture; its archives served as a data bank of St. Lucian music. In brief, RSL served as an avenue for promoting and keeping St. Lucian culture and uniqueness alive.

Still, the prime minister raised some valid arguments for the closure of the station. However, the action does add to the sentiment that the prime minister is ever so keen on discontinuing or dismantling programs or entities that pertain to the heritage of St. Lucians and that speak to who they are as a people.

Citizenship by Investment Program (CIP)

CARICOM territories and countries have always struggled to find economic footing. For a long time, agriculture was the underpinning of these economies. In St. Lucia, the era of green gold, when the banana industry was the mainstay of the economy, was associated with unprecedented socio-economic progress with attendant environmental degradation, health problems, and the vulnerability of a mono-crop economic system. Then it was industrialization, helped along by import substitution theory and Sir Arthur Lewis's dual-sector model of economic development that helped earn him the Nobel Prize for economics and titled him the father of development economics. Under that guise, recognizing Vieux Fort's expanse of flat land, its American ready-made infrastructure, and its airport and seaport facilities, the district was labeled the last frontier and John Compton in his great wisdom attempted to turn the town into the industrial capital of St. Lucia. Then tourism was the craze. So much so that no sooner had Dr. Kenny Anthony come to power in 1997 on the wings of a 16-1 landslide election victory he announced in no uncertain terms that agriculture was out and tourism and services were the in thing. Next, telecommunications took center stage as the instrument of leveling the playing field of economic opportunities and competitiveness. With the help of the World Bank, the telecommunications sector of the Eastern Caribbean was liberalized, the Eastern Caribbean Telecommunications Authority (ECTEL), the world's first multi-country utility regulator, was established to steer the liberalization process.[11] Yet, after all this, the economies of most CARICOM countries continue to flounder with unemployment rates of 15 percent and up.

The search for economic salvation continued.

Now, with St. Kitts and Nevis having led the way, it seems that the Citizenship by Investment Program (CIP) is perceived as the new panacea of CARICOM's economic woes. St. Lucia was not to be left out. In the same way Dr. Kenny Anthony heralded the supremacy of tourism over agriculture, he established the St. Lucia CIP in January 2016, just six months before he would exit government after his party lost the June 2016 general elections. Under the Labour administration, besides processing and due diligence fees, a single applicant had to pay US$200,000 for a St. Lucian citizenship.

When Allen Chastanet came to power, not only did he lower the bar of due diligence and vetting associated with administering the CIP, he cut the CIP fee for a single applicant by half to US$100,000, which meant that St. Lucia, with the largest economy and most diversified manufacturing sector of the Organization of Eastern Caribbean States (OECS),[12] had joined Dominica in offering one of the cheapest citizenships in the world. The prime minister had thus taken CIP down to its lowest denominator, and St. Lucia had become a CIP bottom feeder. With this move, Allen Chastanet may have exposed himself to the criticism that, consistent with his seeming disregard of the country's patrimony, he places a low value on its nationhood, on its citizenship.

Exactly the kind of disposition one would expect of someone who, culturally speaking, is not St. Lucian, and part of what is meant by selling out the country.

Housing and Employment

As mentioned previously, during its fifteen years in government the Kenny Anthony-led SLP administration implemented an unprecedented number of socioeconomic programs aimed at the most vulnerable and economically disadvantaged citizens, in the process being credited with fostering a kinder and gentler country. PROUD (Program for the Regularization of Unplanned Developments), STEP (Short Term Employment Program), and NICE (National Initiative to Create Employment) were three such programs.

PROUD

It must appear odd or ironic to a visitor that while St. Lucia seems keen on donating thousands of acres of land to rich foreigners to build luxury hotels to house strangers, many St. Lucians remain landless. So as a result, in a phenomenon that may be aptly described as "enforced socialism", they have taken matters into their own hands and built their homes (shacks more often than not) on crown lands. And who could blame them? Isn't St. Lucia for St. Lucians?

However, across the island, this has created haphazard and unplanned squatter communities (ghettos might be a fitting description) devoid of such basic infrastructure and amenities as roads, electricity, running water, adequate drainage, and proper garbage collection. Therefore, in 2000, the Labour government introduced PROUD to rationalize these squatter settlements (ghettos) by giving their residents the opportunity to own the land they occupy and providing them with the infrastructure and amenities that other more fortunate communities were enjoying.

STEP

Recognizing the country's persistently high unemployment, in his first term as prime minister, Dr. Kenny Anthony established STEP to provide temporary employment to the neediest of households. STEP workers performed "beautification and de-bushing works" in communities throughout the island. The work program was usually for a few weeks' period and was timed to coincide with when households were under the greatest financial strain, such as when approaching Christmas and toward the beginning of the school year.

NICE

Under NICE, the government took its unemployment busting initiative to a more comprehensive level and implemented a wide range of employment expansion measures, including apprenticeships and training programs for crop production, small engine boat maintenance, multimedia production, customer service office administration and beauty therapy; farm labor support whereby unemployed workers were first trained in agricultural works and then offered employment on "dormant, inactive, or underdeveloped farms"; Christmas private sector employment for students; student summer employment; training for employment in the cruise-ship sector; employment in repairing the homes of elderly citizens; and a program specifically targeting single mothers in which they were employed to provide care to senior citizens who otherwise would have been neglected. The beauty of this program was that it addressed the needs of two vulnerable groups—it created employment among single mothers and improved the quality of life of senior citizens.

The Chastanet Perspective

In addressing the nation on August 7, 2013, as leader of the opposition UWP, Allen Chastanet said that the SLP government suggestion that STEP, NICE, and PROUD have created employment is equivalent to throwing dust in people's eyes, which brings to mind Rick Wayne's more colorful way of saying the same thing—*don't piss in my eyes and call it rain*. In that same address, Allen Chastanet also said that instead of the "happy days" SLP had promised, these programs were tantamount to "Beggar Days."[13] Other detractors characterized the programs as handouts and fostering a culture of dependence. Therefore, no one should have been surprised when the Stephenson King-led UWP government (2006-2011) discontinued STEP (which the Labour government re-instituted upon regaining power in 2011), and that Chastanet either discontinued or scaled down these programs when he took office in 2016.

Chastanet and the UWP are not entirely wrong. STEP, if not PROUD and NICE, seems like a handout. But so does the DSH deal, and the paying of salaries for OJO Labs, and compelling the NIC to loan Cabot Saint Lucia Golf Resort $30 million. The only difference is that these are handouts to millionaire, even billionaire foreigners as opposed to handouts to poor St. Lucians. If so, it would appear that for Chastanet charity begins overseas. This is reminiscent of the US Republicans who, while disparaging welfare assistance to poor Americans, calling black mothers on public assistance "welfare queens", were happy for the government to contribute billions of dollars to farmers (most of them white and many of them wealthy) in the form of price support and land set-aside programs.

Notwithstanding, the Chastanet government failed to appreciate several important considerations.

First. With a perennial unemployment rate of 15 to 25 percent and a youth unemployment rate of over 30 percent, St. Lucia is in a permanent Great Recession or for that matter a permanent Great Depression. This is hardly an exaggeration. During the Great Recession (December 2007 to June 2009) US unemployment rose to only as high as 10.6 percent (in January 2010), and during the Great Depression (1929 to 1941) its unemployment peaked at 25 percent. What did President Franklin D. Roosevelt do to combat the Great Depression? He came up with the New Deal, a series of programs including financial reform, regulations, safety net measures, public works projects, and relief for the unemployed and poor (exactly what Chastanet and some others characterize as handouts and dependency). Since the New Deal, the US has not had to face an economic downturn as severe as the Great Depression. It would appear that the Chastanet government and all previous St. Lucia administrations have failed to appreciate that, based on unemployment statistics, St. Lucia is in a perpetual Great Depression.

Second. The marginal propensity to consume (MPC), which is the proportion of additional income that is spent on consumption, is a well-known economic concept. Economists have established that low-income households have a higher MPC than their high-income counterparts, meaning, compared to rich households, poor households spend (as opposed to saving) a larger proportion of any additional income. This makes intuitive sense because, since poor households are living hand to mouth, they are likely to spend most of any additional income that comes their way. On the other hand, the basic needs of rich households are already being met, so they can be expected to save a larger percentage of any additional income. Many of the persons employed under STEP and NICE are from low-income households, therefore they are likely to spend most of the income earned from these programs.

In economics, the multiplier effect is the impact of an initial injection into the economy on increases in economic activity. The greater the MPC, the larger the multiplier effect. Thus, one can expect the ultimate impact of STEP and NICE on increases in economic activity (multiplier effect) to be much greater than the income the workers received. One can also expect STEP and NICE workers to spend a lot of their earnings in their own communities, thus stimulating economic activity (considering the multiplier effect) in economically depressed areas.

Third. PROUD turned squatters into legitimate land and home owners, and this is no insignificant matter. Land and homeownership imbue persons with a sense of belonging, permanence, solidity. It gives them a stake in their community and in their country, therefore they are more likely to engage in protecting and improving their neighborhood, and to take part in community activities and in the political process. In brief, homeownership produces more empowered, proactive, and responsible citizens. Moreover, homeownership can improve the economic standing of families in that real estate can facilitate the acquisition of loans for starting or expanding businesses and for financing education and training.

Fourth. It is important to understand that many adults in chronically underprivileged and economically depressed areas (because they lack the requisite work habits and social and literacy skills), have become unemployable, especially regarding structured or formal employment. Therefore, no matter how many hotels, call centers, factories, etc., that come to town, many of these persons will remain jobless. This means, though temporary, STEP was providing employment to persons who otherwise are locked out of the formal economy, the structured job market.

Laptops

In 2013 the Labour government introduced the one-laptop-per-child program that equipped every Form Three and Four secondary school student with a laptop. In its first year (2013) the program was sponsored by the government of Trinidad and Tobago, and in its second and third years it was sponsored, respectively, by the governments of Venezuela and Taiwan. By the time the Labour Party bowed out of power in June 2016, it had provided students, teachers, and secondary schools with about 15,000 laptops, 525 desktops, and 125 projectors. And thanks to the generosity of the OAS and the government of Taiwan, it had provided training to hundreds of teachers on integrating ICT in the classroom.

When the UWP came to power in 2016, it discontinued the one-laptop-per-child program, offering as rationale such pronouncements as: "People cannot eat laptops"; and "It is not enough to give a child a laptop."[14] Statements that seem almost as callous as the one attributed to Marie-Antoinette, bride of France's King Louis XVI, who, when told that her subjects had no bread, supposedly replied with "Qu'ils mangent de la brioche" — "Let them eat cake."[15]

The one-laptop-per-child program was not without problems. It was reported that some students and their families abused the computers, the operating system of some laptops was incompatible with windows software, school WIFI and internet access were unreliable and of insufficient bandwidth, teachers and students were inadequately trained or ill-prepared to take full advantage of the initiative, there were no provisions for software licensing, and insufficient attention was given to the maintenance and servicing of the computers.[16]

These problems would have reduced the efficacy of the program, so maybe this is why the UWP government had downplayed its usefulness or necessity However, in a country where many parents cannot afford school bus fare and can barely provide their children with one proper meal per day, the program may have represented the only chance of many secondary school students gaining ready access to computers, which some would argue is an essential and not an optional educational requirement in this rapidly information and communication technology changing world. Having forced schools to shift from brick and motor facilities to online platforms, COVID-19 has further emphasized the importance of students owning computers and tablets.

George Charles, St. Lucia's first post-universal suffrage chief-executive or head of government, can be credited with politically enfranchising St. Lucians. John Compton can be credited with building the country's physical and economic infrastructure. Dr. Kenny Anthony can be credited with advancing the country's social infrastructure (health, sports, education, culture, amenities) and in so doing created a kinder and gentler country. If Allen Chastanet's first term in office is an indication of his modus operandi, one wonders what historians will credit him with? Will they credit him with playing Robin Hood in reverse — robbing poor St. Lucians to enrich wealthy foreigners? The jury is still out.

10

DISREGARD FOR THE LAWS OF THE LAND

A fourth accusation levied on the Chastanet-led UWP government is that it is running roughshod over the laws and statutory institutions of the country. If so, what are some of the episodes or actions that have incited this allegation.

The NURC

The National Utilities Regulatory Commission (NURC) was established by the 2011 Kenny Anthony Labour government through the National Utilities Regulatory Commission Act (2016) to regulate the supply of utility services, including water and electricity. The Water and Sewerage Company (WASCO), a quasi-statutory body, is the main supplier of the country's potable water, while St. Lucia Electricity Services Limited (LUCELEC) is the principal supplier of electricity. The operations of the NURC secretariat were supervised by a commission comprising seven commissioners appointed by the Labour government. When the Chastanet-led UWP came to power, Stephenson King, the minister responsible for public utilities, revoked the appointments of the commissioners in June 2018, citing misconduct as the reason for the revocations. The NURC's Act details the conditions under which the minister can revoke the appointments of commissioners. Misconduct is one of these conditions.[1,2]

What was the misconduct? The failure of the Commission to carry out the minister's directive of not renewing the contract of the NURC's executive director to be replaced by a new commissioner who would double as commissioner and executive director. However, fairness and a reading of the NURC's Act suggest that the Commission would have been derelict in its duties and responsibilities and in violation of the law were it to comply with the minister's directive.

First, section 8 of the Act provides that the minister may issue directives to the Commission of a general policy nature. However, it is reasonable to surmise that the staffing of the NURC secretariat is not of a general policy nature, rather it is an administrative matter and therefore falls outside the purview of the minister.

Second, the Act does not envision the commissioner-executive position that the minister wished to impose. Therefore, such a change would violate the law of the country.

Third, the Act makes specific provisions for a position of executive director, separate from the role of commissioner, who along with other staff are to be appointed by the Commission. The Act makes no provisions for a commissioner-executive director and makes no provisions for the minister to appoint staff or to give directives to the Commission in the appointment of staff.

Fourth, the commissioners could find few faults with the executive director. They maintained that his conduct, performance, leadership, communication, and pro-activeness were without reproach. For example, his performance evaluation yielded an approval score of over 90 percent. Consequently, the Commission felt that it had no grounds for failing to renew the contract of the executive director, and failure of renewal would have been unfair and tantamount to penalizing excellence.

Therefore, in issuing directives to the Commission in matters of staffing, the minister was operating outside the provisions of the NURC's Act, which governs the operations and conduct of the Commission. It also appears that were the Commission to carry out the directive of the minister, not only would the Commission be in breach of the Act but would be complicit in the minister unlawfully usurping its authority and responsibilities.

It is not by accident that the Act refrains from making provisions for the minister to meddle in the staffing and other administrative affairs of the secretariat and that the Act spells out the conditions under which the minister can revoke the appointments of commissioners and that, unlike the directors of most Boards, commissioners cannot be summarily dismissed with a change of administration. All this is to ensure that the Commission dispense its regulatory responsibilities with independence, impartiality, and the absence of undue political influence or interference. The minister's wrongful revocation of the commissioners' appointments was exactly what the framers of the NURC Act were trying to prevent when instead of a Board they established a Commission.

One can safely say that the minister was very much aware of the foregoing regulatory principles and stipulations of the Act and thus knew that the Commission could not lawfully carry out his directive. Therefore, one has to conclude that the minister's directive was a guise to get rid of a Labour government-appointed Commission and an executive director appointed by same Commission, knowing full well that the commissioners would rather resign than violate the trust and responsibilities vested in them.

Perhaps the ultimate reason the minister sought to dismiss the Commission was that in carrying out its regulatory oversight and protecting the public's interest, the Commission was perceived as preventing WASCO from conducting business as usual, which may suggest that the minister was in cahoots with the public utility company. Clearly, such motivation by the minister reeks of corruption and would be tantamount to him placing the interest of the public utilities above that of citizens (hence economic extraction) and returning the public utilities to self-regulation.

The NURC incident presents an obvious example of the Chastanet-led UWP government violating the laws of the country and undermining the integrity of its statutory institutions. Therefore, who could blame Chastanet's detractors for viewing such blatant disregard for the laws and statutory bodies of the nation as a slippery slope to a dysfunctional and despotic country?

The National Trust

According to the St. Lucia National Trust, on September 6, 2018, its officers became aware through social media that the government was about to demolish the historical Royal Gaol prison and affiliated structures to make way for the police headquarters and criminal courts. Built in 1827, the Royal Gaol is the oldest known structure in St. Lucia, the oldest known standing structure in the Castries city center, and one of the few remaining artifacts of the slavery era. Also, at the time of the Royal Gaol's construction, it was considered one of the most significant structures in Castries and one of the best jails in the West Indies.[3]

Recognizing the historical, architectural, and cultural importance of the Royal Gaol, and mindful of its mandate to preserve the natural and cultural patrimony of the country, the Trust immediately and successfully petitioned the High Court to place an injunction on the demolition in progress. Because of the injunction, government officials had little choice but to meet with the Trust to discuss the way forward. The series of meetings that ensued culminated in the signing of an agreement between the Trust and the government whereby the government would cease the demolition of the Royal Gaol and related structures until consultation between the Trust and the government on the development of the old prison were concluded and consideration given to the recommendations of the Trust.[3]

Secure in the knowledge that through consultation and acceptance of its recommendations the Royal Gaol building would be incorporated into the design of the police headquarters and criminal courts, the Trust withdrew its legal challenge and hence the court rescinded the injunction.

However, with the injunction discharged, never bothering to consult with the Trust much less obtain its recommendations, on Saturday, May 23, 2020, without notice to the National Trust, the government unceremoniously demolished the historic Royal Gaol building.

The Royal Gaol was an abandoned, unused, and deteriorating structure, so maybe in the eyes of Chastanet and his colleagues it was a useless nuisance that needed to be demolished. Nonetheless, a government more committed to preserving the country's patrimony, and more willing to invest in the notion of nationhood, may have taken the opportunity to not only incorporate the Royal Gaol into the new building configuration but to give the Royal Gaol a facelift and transform it from a seemingly useless building to a historical and cultural attraction, thereby enhancing the appeal of the building complex.

The agreement between the Trust and the government led the Trust to discharge the court injunction, therefore by reneging on the agreement the government violated the spirit of the law. In effect it used trickery to defy a court order. The government's transgression can be viewed as disrespecting, sabotaging, and demoralizing a statutory institution for doing exactly what the laws of the country required of it. The government was thus punishing good behavior and providing disincentives to doing the right thing, to doing what was in the best interest of the country.

Even the most diehard UWP and Chastanet supporter must have felt the anguish of the Trust when, reacting to the government's violation of the signed agreement, it said:[3]

> The Government of Saint Lucia openly and blatantly demonstrated its disregard for the rule of law, our patrimony, good governance and integrity in public office. The Government of Saint Lucia and the holders of its highest offices showed that they cannot be trusted when they enter into negotiations and execute agreements and undertakings, demonstrating a lack of moral leadership and integrity. By their actions they have demonstrated their utter contempt for Fair Helen's patrimony and the things that uniquely make us Saint Lucian. This flagrant and wanton destruction of who we are as a people is sadly an indelible stain on all Saint Lucians and should not be accepted by anyone who truly loves Saint Lucia.

Regarding Cabot Saint Lucia, which was cited earlier, the National Trust has another fight on its hands. Other than an initial meeting at which the developer agreed to implement the development in accordance with international best practice and to engage the Trust in ongoing dialog on the best way forward, the developer refused to meet with the Trust and to address some of its environmental concerns. Meantime, according to the Trust,[4] the development has proceeded without monitoring and environmental safeguards and without conducting an impact assessment study. Conceptual plans reveal that part of the development will be built over known Amerindian burial sites. Excavation has unearthed archeological artifacts and is threatening the area's biodiversity and fragile coastal ecosystem. For example, the land clearing is endangering the wide variety of cacti found on the site's Cactus Valley. And, according to marine biologist, Jeannine Compton-Antoine, [5] without mitigation measures the clear-cutting and removal of ground cover are likely to cause significant run-off that will no doubt "smother" the seabed's coral reef system, thus endangering the marine population (green-back turtles for example) and the livelihoods of fisherfolk.

The National Trust and many concerned citizens are also perturbed that the development is likely to include the Queen's Chain. If so, public access to the seashore may be cut off, thereby denying St. Lucians the use of the beach. A selling point of the development to potential clients is that it will provide exclusive access to the beach. And as proof, the developer has already started to block access to the seashore, and government has approved a lease of the Queen's Chain to Cabot Saint Lucia for 75 years.[6]

Yet the seashore in question is not an isolated, sparsely used area. Being close to the Castries-Gros Islet metropolis, the island's most densely populated corridor, accounting for over half of the population (55 percent), it is heavily used by St. Lucians and visitors alike for several activities including sea bathing, beach picnics, walking and hiking, camping, bird watching, fishing, biodiversity conservation and study, safari tours, horseback riding, kite surfing, and restaurants and bars.

The Queen's Chain is the part of the seashore extending 186.5 feet from the established high-water line. A traditional and long-held interpretation of the constitution and ordinances of St. Lucia is that the only allowable development on the Queen's Chain are those involving public works, embellishment, and defense (which clearly excludes hotel and golf course development); and that the Queen's Chain is the inviolable property of the state and hence that of all St. Lucians and therefore cannot be legally

sold or leased, and the public cannot be denied access to it.[7,8] If
so, the government lease of the Queen's Chain to Cabot St. Lucia
and its sanction of the development's use of the beach at the exclusion of St. Lucians represents yet another instance of the
prime minister violating the laws and ordinances of the country.

Some government ministers and UWP supporters have in-
sinuated that the Trust is anti-UWP and is seeking to impede the
administration's development initiatives. However, as the Trust
has intimated, previous administrations have worked hand in
hand with it to ensure that developments adhere to international
best practice and adopt measures to protect the country's historical,
cultural, and natural patrimony. Thus, in sharp contrast to the
current administration's constant attempts to frustrate and
preclude the Trust from the development process, other administrations had taken it as a given that the Trust must be involved
and that developers must address the Trust's concerns.

Governments have only five years to get things done and impress voters that they deserve additional terms. So one can be
certain that project delays due to the Trust's involvement have
frustrated not just developers but a government or two. One can
also be certain governments have turned a blind eye to the
covert and not so covert strategies that hotels have employed to
frustrate St. Lucians from accessing the beaches adjoining their
property, and governments have been quite aware that some
hotels have situated themselves alongside isolated coves in such
a way that the only ready access to the beach is by sea or through
their property, thereby effectively precluding public access to
the beach.

However, in the eyes of SLP supporters and many concerned
citizens, Chastanet's UWP administration is the first government
that has openly precluded the Trust from getting involved with
a development, and that has overtly teamed up with a developer
to deny St. Lucians their inalienable rights to access the island's

beaches. If so, can one blame St. Lucians for accusing Chastanet of favoring foreigners at their expense?

The DCA

The Development Control Authority (DCA) is responsible for approving applications for land development in St. Lucia. A Cabinet appointed board comprising thirteen directors from various government agencies supervises the operations of the DCA. The Physical Planning and Development Act (2001)[9] stipulates that "a person shall not commence or carry out the development of any land in St. Lucia without the prior written permission of the head of the Physical Planning and Development Division," i.e., the head of DCA.

It would appear that the Physical Planning and Development Act applies only to private entities and not to government. Because apparently UWP administrations have made a habit of sanctioning land and construction developments without DCA approval. Untold Stories,[10] an investigative journalism television talk show, revealed that the rebuilding of St. Jude's Hospital (which started under the Stephenson King UWP government) after the 2009 fire had ravaged the facility, was executed without DCA approval and without government-approved building plans. Likewise, based on the Trust's press release on the Royal Gaol misadventure, it is doubtful that the government had secured DCA approval for land development before demolishing the structures and engaging in site preparation. The DCA could not furnish DSH development plans upon request, suggesting that the development started without DCA approval. Cabot Saint Lucia represents yet another development that has proceeded without conducting the DCA required impact assessment study. Apparently, in cahoots with the developer and the government, DCA refused to meet with the Trust to discuss the Cabot development and frustrated the Trust's efforts to obtain pertinent information on the project. Therefore, not only does Chastanet's government blatantly violate the laws of the country but poisons state institutions to follow suit.

Maybe in their rush to start and complete projects, other administrations have also disregarded the DCA and started projects without the agency's approval. The Cabinet of the ruling administration appoints the DCA board of directors, therefore it should surprise no one if they were to overlook the transgressions of the government. Moreover, minister Stephenson King's illegal dismissal of the NURC commission serves as a reminder of the ruthlessness of governments toward statutory bodies that get in their way. According to Untold Stories, when the Kenny Anthony Labour government took over the rebuilding of St. Jude's from the former administration, several new buildings were added to the configuration but at no point was there DCA approval or government approved building plans.

Other administrations may have violated the stipulations of the Physical Planning and Development Act and may have even defied other statutes, but some would argue that the Chastanet-led UWP government stands apart in the frequency and brazenness in which it disregards the laws of the land and corrupts or undermines its statutory institutions. A pattern more aligned with a despotism than with a democracy ruled by law.

11

MODUS OPERANDI

The fifth criticism of the Chastanet government refers to the way it conducts business. The government is accused of a management style that lacks transparency and accountability. Its policies are said to be incoherent and directionless. Rather than following a well-devised plan of action, the government is seen as simply blundering along. Some have even expressed the sickening feeling that the government is set on deceiving the populace. Serious accusations indeed. Once again, the discussion turns to the evidence to ascertain the plausibility of such claims.

Betrayal

First, the demolition of the Royal Gaol. As mentioned above, the government signed an agreement with the St. Lucia National Trust that it will wait after consultations were concluded and consideration given to the Trust's recommendations before resuming the demolition. With this guarantee, the Trust withdrew its legal challenge to the demolition and as a result the courts lifted the injunction. However, with the injunction lifted, awaiting no further consultations with the Trust, much less its recommendations, the government hastily demolished the buildings. So who can blame the Trust and others critical of the government that it uses deception to get away with flouting the laws of the land and that seems to be part of its modus operandi.

Subterfuge

The underhand (and some would say bogus) manner in which the government revoked the appointments of the NURC commissioners when they refused to carry out the misguided instructions of the minister, which would have been a breach of the NURC's Act and would have rendered the commissioners complicit in the minister unlawfully usurping the Commission's authority and responsibilities, can be viewed as another data point in this the government's modus operandi.

Duplicity

Coinciding with the Chastanet-led UWP government, Fresh Start, a little-known construction company, was reported to be the recipient of a significant share of large government contracts, many of them by direct award. Meaning, Fresh Start won the contracts without participating in a bidding process. This, by itself, would have raised the eyebrows of SLP supporters and other concerned citizens. But in July 2020 a Cabinet order, which was leaked and circulated, stipulated that, under the Fiscal Incentives Act, government gave Fresh Start a 100 percent, three-year income tax holiday; 100 percent waiver of import duty and excise tax on pickup vans and SUV vehicles; and 100 percent waiver of excise tax on concrete mixer equipment and trucks.[1]

On HTS News, former independent senator, Everistus Jn Marie, lamented that the incentives provided to Fresh Start are "troubling, an abuse of power, and illegal." Illegal because the

Fiscal Incentives Act does not envision providing concessions to construction companies, and it is outside the powers of Cabinet to decide which services qualify for concessions.

The senator said: "What was the most disturbing for me was the waiver of income tax, very troubling, sinister, and suggests something a lot bigger. Because having been granted a contract without having to compete for it, you now saying to that entity you don't even have to pay your dues to society in terms of taxes. That is wrong." According to the senator, this kind of modus operandi is "creating a culture of illegality and corruption...it will impoverish us...and it will create crime... and it's about time politicians pay with their freedom (prison sentences) for acting that way."[2]

The PAJOAH Letter Scandal

The PAJOAH letter scandal, as revealed by the media and the opposition SLP, may represent yet another data point in the government's modus operandi.

A letter[3] bearing the letterhead of the government of St. Lucia and the stamp of the Ministry of Economic Development, Transport and Civil Aviation, apparently signed by Guy Joseph, minister for the said ministry, and addressed "to whom it may concern," specified that the government "has agreed to enter a contractual relationship with PAJOAH's Limited" whereby the government would repay a loan of US$62 million (EC$167.4 million) at 3.5 percent interest over 15 years for two projects — the St Jude Hospital rebuilding project and a street lighting project that supposedly had already been financed by the Caribbean Development Bank.

Apparently, according to established ministerial code of conduct and international best practice, only the prime minister can authorize a letter pledging such government commitment. Yet the prime minister denied knowledge of the letter much less admitting to authorizing it. If the prime minister is to be believed, according to SLP opposition leader, Philip J. Pierre,[4] this leaves only two scenarios. Either someone forged the signature of Guy Joseph or the minister had taken it upon himself to unlawfully commit the government to a contractual agreement with PAJOAH. Pierre said that if the latter, this represented "gross misbehavior in public office .... a clear breach of the protocols, checks and balances as pertains to matters of public finance," therefore disciplinary action must be taken against the offending minister, including dismissal from public office.

Pierre demanded that the prime minister conduct a full investigation and get to the bottom of the matter. But his plea fell on deaf ears, for not only did the prime minister refuse to launch an inquiry, it took him (according to Pierre) over three months to even question Guy Joseph about the authenticity of the letter.

Interestingly, and even comically, Guy Joseph never categorically denied or confirmed writing and signing the letter; instead, he turned to what appears to be another dimension of the government's modus operandi when faced with accusations of mismanagement or official wrong-doing. Like a rude and brazen child caught with his hand in the cookie jar, the minister made light of the accusation by ridiculing the notion that the letter was a breach of ministerial code and that it warranted his resignation. Then he deflected the allegations by insinuating that the former SLP governments of which Pierre was part had been guilty of much more serious breaches than the PAJOAH letter, yet no one was ever disciplined or discharged from office.[3] From this reaction, it would appear that to Guy Joseph the business of government, the business of the nation, is a big joke. Then can one be blamed for pronouncing the Allen Chastanet - Guy Joseph led UWP government the worst in St. Lucia's history?

Like most other persons in public office, it is almost impossible to get politicians to openly admit to wrongdoing. On that score, the comment by Dr. Ubaldus Raymond, a former minister in the

Chastanet administration, on a talk show television program is telling. He reportedly said: "If we have to go down that road, not one of the parliamentarians can stand, not one who can stand. There are those who will do their stuff and are doing their stuff and will never be caught. In fact, some of them have done criminal stuff."[5]

So one would be naive to expect Guy Joseph to suddenly and openly confess his role in the PAJOAH letter. Therefore, to approach or arrive at the truth, one may need to read between the lines, pay attention to what was said and what was not said, and discern patterns of behavior. In that regard, given the minister never denied wrongdoing, and the fact that he prefaced his innuendos of SLP misconduct with "two wrongs do not make a right,"[3] he may have inadvertently admitted to his culpability in the PAJOAH letter. If the minister is culpable, the next question is, to what end? What was the minister to gain by acting in deceit and risking condemnation that he would violate a well-established and internationally accepted code of conduct? Moreover, should one believe that the prime minister was not a party to the scheme, whatever it may be?

Bribery

In terms of pattern of behavior, let us see what tracks minister Guy Joseph and prime minister Allen Chastanet have left behind.

The initial airfield in Vieux Fort, called Beanfield Airport, was built by the Americans as part of their World War II military installations when they transformed Vieux Fort and surrounding areas into a military base. In the 1970s, Seroc, a Canadian construction company, extended the airstrip to accommodate long-range intercontinental commercial aircraft. The airfield was pronounced an international airport and renamed Hewanorra, a bastardization of Iouanalao, the Amerindian name for the island, meaning "land of the iguana". Since then the airport has become the gateway to St. Lucia, the main point of entry for its tourists and thus a vital plank in its all-important tourism industry.

In recent years, both St. Lucia's major political parties, though at butt heads on most issues, are in agreement that Hewanorra International is overdue for expansion and upgrade. During the reign of the Stephenson King-led UWP administration (2006-2011), the government started pursuing the redevelopment of Hewanorra International Airport, estimated to cost US157 million, or at the time roughly 12 percent of the country's gross domestic product (GDP).

In 2009 the St. Lucia Air and Sea Ports Authority (SLASPA), the custodian of the airport, opened the bidding process for contracting the airport redevelopment project. Among the three finalists was the Asphalt and Mining Company (A&M) run by Antonio Assenza, a South Floridian businessman who apparently had prior connections with Guy Joseph, then minister for communications, works, transport and public utilities. Earlier, upon the minister's alleged request, A&M was awarded two multi-million dollar contracts, namely the Babonneau Highway (EC$12.24 million) and Desruisseaux Road (EC$10.55 million) rehabilitation projects. Not only were the contracts direct purchases, meaning they were awarded without advertising and competitive bidding, but later they were found to be significantly overpriced.[6]

Regarding the airport redevelopment project, both Dr. Kenny Anthony and Richard Frederick (then Guy Joseph's colleague in Cabinet), accused Guy Joseph of attempted bribery. They reported that he had offered prime minister Stephenson King EC$5 million if he would sign to award the contract to A&M, and EC$1 million to Richard Frederick to help convince the prime minister to take the bait. Apparently, both men refused the bribe and King did not sign the proposed contract because SLASPA's recommendations to Cabinet ranked A&M's bid proposal last of the three finalists.[7,8] But it seems Guy Joseph had refused to take no for an answer, for later in the year SLASPA notified the three finalists that their bids were unsuccessful and reopened the bidding process. This second time around, Guy Joseph and A&M prevailed. SLASPA recommended A&M's proposal as the winning bid, and in February 2010 the government awarded the project to A&M. However, the project fell through because the Deutsche Bank from which St. Lucia was seeking part of the finance for the initiative denied the request due (partly) to the failure of Antonio Assenza to pass its diligence test.[6]

Meantime, general elections came along in 2011, and the Kenny Anthony-led Labour Party regained power. The Labour government hired Bob Lindquist, a forensic accountant, to help investigate the award of the airport redevelopment project during the UWP administration for any criminal wrongdoing. Under the Mutual Legal Assistance Treaty, the Labour government also requested the assistance of the US Justice Department to help investigate the matter. The US found the evidence of probable criminality compelling enough to launch an independent investigation. The case was filed in a South Florida court. Guy Joseph along with Antonio Assenza, Andre Edgar (a businessman in St. Lucia), Sean Matthew (former head of SLASPA), and Allen Chastanet (then minister for tourism) were all mentioned in the US investigation.[6]

However, before the inquiries could make headway, elections came along again (in 2016) and this time around the victor was the UWP led by Allen Chastanet. Alarmed of the US involvement in the case, prime minister Allen Chastanet and Guy Joseph, now minister for economic development, transport and civil aviation, reportedly sought the help of an associate with connections in South Florida to sway Florida politicians in Washington to inhibit the investigation.[9]

Unsurprisingly, given a UWP government with a disincentive to continue the inquiry, the investigation came to a halt. Allen Chastanet said it all when he promised to "investigate the investigation." Guy Joseph felt so smug and secure that he said the investigation will continue and it will prove his innocence. And so the Hewanorra Airport Redevelopment scandal became yet another data point in the UWP's perceived modus operandi and Guy Joseph's pattern of apparent deceit and corruption.[9,10]

Although both the SLP and UWP concur on the necessity of redeveloping Hewanorra International, they differ on the means of doing so. As indicated in Part I, the Kenny Anthony Labour government preferred option was to privatize the operations of the airport in a Public Private Partnership (PPP) arrangement involving a private entity that would redevelop, operate and maintain the airport. SLASPA would be relegated to the role of regulating the operator, and the government would collect corporate taxes and receive a share of corporate profits. With the PPP, the government would avoid borrowing money and increasing its debt burden, and as a professional outfit specializing in airport concessions, the private entity is likely to be more effective than SLASPA in increasing airport traffic flow and operating the airport efficiently and profitably. Despite these benefits and the fact that PPP is becoming the international best practice for operating airports (and it was not clear that SLASPA was running the airport at a profit), the Chastanet government scoffed at the idea of a PPP, saying in effect why should the government give away such a vital asset for a foreign entity to profit from when the government can do the honors and keep all the profits?[11]

On the surface, the political parties' differing approaches to the redevelopment of the airport can be attributed to philosophical or conceptual differences. But given the alleged attempted bribery and the awarding of the contract to A&M after placing last among the finalists in the initial bidding process, one wonders whether the UWP's rejection of the PPP approach was less a matter of philosophy and more a matter of ulterior motives. Meaning, as opposed to the government being intimately involved in the project's construction and having business connections with potential contractors (which creates opportunities for bribery and kickbacks), the PPP approach, which would invariably involve global airport concession companies with which government officials would have little connections, may offer fewer opportunities for personal gain, for economic extraction. A view opposition leader, Philip J. Pierre, echoed when he said:

> It must be clear to all close observers of what is taking place in the health sector and other areas of government activity in the country, that decisions are based on creating as many opportunities as possible for contracts to be issued without tendering. It is also natural and reasonable for the public to speculate as to what special benefits are being derived by persons associated with the Government which consistently handpicks private entities to award contracts without an open tendering process.[12]

Clearly, if all the scandal accusations against Guy Joseph turn out to be factual, then Guy Joseph may be a candidate for the most corrupt politician in St. Lucia's history, and by implication the Chastanet-led UWP administration may be a candidate for the most corrupt government. Then is it any wonder that an online poll,[13] conducted by State of Urgency in August/September 2020 on St. Lucian's perception of the country's "socio-political" landscape, ranked corruption as the third most critical issue facing the country, behind unemployment and quality of leadership, but before crime, healthcare, education, the economy, national debt, cost of living, political division, and climate change?

12

IT'S THE ECONOMY, STUPID

In 2016 Allen Chastanet ran on an election platform in which he would manage the country as a business and as a businessman he would roll up his sleeves and get to work. This was politically astute of Chastanet not only because the stance contrasted sharply with the perception that Dr. Kenny Anthony took too long to get things done but also because economic issues usually feature strongly in voters' choice of political parties or candidates, i.e., who they think are more likely to bring home the bacon usually wins the election. As confirmation of the importance of economic issues to St. Lucian voters, the results of the previously mentioned State of Urgency online poll, ranked unemployment (first) and the economy (fourth) as among the most critical issues facing the country. So, besides a look at UWP's modus operandi, it may be useful to examine how well Chastanet has fared compared to former prime ministers based on unemployment, economic growth, and other socioeconomic variables as public debt and crime.

The data for the analysis is presented in Table 1. The unemployment rate, real GDP growth rate, and homicide rate (homicides

Table 1.

Comparison of Administrations based on Socioeconomic Indicators

Administration	Unemployment Rate[1,2]	Real GDP Growth Rate[3]	% Change Public Dept GDP Ratio[4]	Ave Annual Number of Homicides[5]	Homicide Rate[5]
Compton UWP (82 -87)		8.2			
Compton UWP (87-92)		7.4			
Compton-Lewis UWP (92-97)	17.2	3.0	20.3	12.2	8.3
Anthony SLP (97 - 01)	19.3	1.0	42.8	20.0	12.8
Anthony SLP (01 - 06)	19.6	3.6	23.8	39.8	24.5
King UWP (06 - 11)	15.6	2.0	14.2	39.4	23.0
Anthony SLP (11 - 16)	22.1	0.5	11.0	32.8	18.6
Chastanet UWP (16 - 19)	20.9	2.8	7.5	43.3	24.2

per 100k population) for each administrative term (normally 5 years) were obtained as the average of the annual rates. The change in the ratio of public debt to GDP was computed as the change in the ratio from the previous government and is meant to capture growth in public debt realized under each administration.

As a caveat please note that the exercise is not meant to be a formal evaluation of the performances of the administrations, for such an evaluation would involve much more than simply comparing the statistics presented in Table 1. For example, a comparison would need to account for the many factors — natural and manmade disasters, external shocks, COVID-19, etc., — beyond the control of government that would have significantly affected the economic performance of the country. The evaluation may also need to consider that there is usually a time lag between implementing government policies/actions and when the results of these policies/actions are realized, and the implication that an administration can inherit the benefits/injuries of the policies/actions of a previous administration.

Thankfully, the aim here is much less ambitious. SLP and its supporters are insistent that Chastanet must go, and appear to be threatening voters with the Chastanet Ultimatum. Some have said that the Allen Chastanet UWP government is the worst in the history of the country. So the task at hand is simply to take a casual look at the socioeconomic data to see if it is so far worse than that of previous administrations to warrant SLP's view (on socioeconomic grounds) of the Chastanet government.

According to the Table, during the first four years of the Chastanet administration (2016 to 2019), the country registered an average annual unemployment rate of 20.9 percent, which is lower than the 22.1 percent experienced under the previous (SLP) administration, but higher than those of the rest of the featured administrations.

On average, the gross domestic product (GDP) expanded by 2.8 percent under the current government, a growth significantly higher than that of the Kenny Anthony-led SLP first (1 percent) and third (0.5 percent) administrations, and higher than the 2 percent realized during the Stephenson King UWP government.

Regarding the debt to GDP ratio, the Chastanet administration cannot be accused of being less prudent than other administrations in managing the country's debt, at least regarding debt to GDP. The debt to GDP ratio has increased by 7.5 percent, from 66.6 when Chastanet assumed office to 71.6 at the end of 2019. This increase is substantially smaller than obtained under the other featured administrations. However, bear in mind that the data does not include the last year (2020/2021) of Chastanet's administration.

The Chastanet administration registered an annual average of 43.3 murders, the highest among all featured administrations, the next closest being the 39.8 annual average murders committed during the 2001-2006 Kenny Anthony government. Its homicide rate of 24.2 ranked it second only to the 24.5 rate observed during the reign of the former Kenny Anthony SLP government.

This brief exercise suggests that on economic grounds the Chastanet government is not the worst St. Lucia has had. In terms of economic growth, the administration has held its own. However, it should be a concern that the government leads other administrations in average annual number of homicides, and, with 27 murders by July 31, the 2020 homicide count was on track to match the 51 homicides reported in 2019, which would push the murder rate of the Chastanet government above that of any previous administration.

Based on this analysis one will have to conclude that the economic evidence does not support the suspicion that the Chastanet-led UWP government is the worst in the history of the country, and the crime situation is not sufficiently worse than that of the former administration to warrant the statement.

Of course, as discussed in Chapters 7 to 11, the story changes considerably when one looks at the government's seeming modus operandi of deceit, duplicity, bribery, and corruption; its tendency to disregard the laws and statutory bodies of the land and to putting the interest of foreigners above that of its citizens; its seeming debasing of the populace; and its dismissiveness of the country's patrimony. The discussion seems to suggest that on those grounds the Chastanet-led UWP government stands apart from other administrations, and therefore SLP supporters and other concerned citizens are not without cause for insisting that Chastanet must go and for regarding his government as the worst in the history of St. Lucia.

13

THE COMPTON DEFICIENCY

The preceding chapters suggest that the perception of many St. Lucians that the Allen Chastanet administration is the worst in St. Lucia's history is not unfounded. Therefore, they can hardly be blamed for remonstrating that the country can ill afford another five years of an Allen Chastanet-led UWP government and so Chastanet-must-go.

Looking at this seemingly sad state of UWP affairs, many Flambeau stalwarts must be moaning about how far their mighty political party has fallen. The party that ruled St. Lucia for an unprecedented three (almost) continuous decades. The party that ushered and shepherded the island into statehood and independence. The party that oversaw the transformation of the country from a sugar plantocracy (an extractive economic institution that spoke of slavery) to a democratizing banana industry that set off a social, political and economic revolution; and then to a broad-based agricultural, manufacturing and tourism economy, making it the country with the largest economy (based on GDP) and most diversified manufacturing industry in the OECS.[1] A party which, according to social historian, Dr.

Jolien Harmsen, "transformed poor, down-trodden, proletarian sugar workers into a middle class of prosperous farming entrepreneurs."[2] The party whose supreme leader, Sir John Compton, was the first and only premier of St. Lucia and its first and longest-serving prime minister, in the process earning himself a knighthood and gaining such accolades as a great visionary, the Father of the Nation, and of whom, Rick Wayne, St. Lucia's most famous journalist and world-renowned body builder, said, "...no one comes even close to deserving more than John Compton the high honor of being declared St. Lucia's Man of the Century."[3]

So far the discussion has looked at how a well-organized and functioning incumbent Labour Party lost the 2016 elections to a disintegrating UWP led by a political novice with plenty going against him. So maybe it's time to look at how the UWP switched from having at its helm arguably the best head of government in the country's history to seemingly the worst one? And, in this inquiry, it may be useful to go to the very beginning and look at John Compton, the man who started it all.

When John Compton returned to St. Lucia in 1952 with a University of Oxford degree in law and economics, he found a country on the move—three labor unions were in operation, Universal Adult Suffrage was yesteryear's news, and the island's two political parties, the St. Lucia Labour Party and the People's Progressive Party had already contested a general election. George Charles and his brothers in the struggle were on a high. Any and everything seemed possible. While they were forging a political revolution of sorts, the banana industry was about to set off a social and economic revolution, and, led by Dunstan St. Omer and the Walcott brothers, the St. Lucia Arts Guild was unleashing a renaissance, a cultural revolution.[4]

In that euphoric atmosphere, both the St. Lucia Workers Union and the St. Lucia Labour Party were more than welcoming of fresh and talented men who could help in the struggle. So, unaware of Compton's weakness of having to be in charge, and unsuspecting that the very cause of his joy would later cause him great grief, referring to the arrival of John Compton and Maurice Mason from their studies, George Charles, then chief minister, wrote: "The Labour Movement heralded this youthful and professional injection with enthusiasm and Messrs. Compton and Mason were quickly embraced in the leadership."[5]

The first clue to Compton's personality tic of needing to do the dictating rather than being dictated to, and possessing an inability or unwillingness to work with persons well-positioned or well equipped to challenge his leadership, which George Charles should have taken as a signal of his imminent challenge for the leadership of the Labour Party and the country, came in 1954 as the Labour Party was positioning itself to contest the second post-Universal Adult Suffrage general elections. For this election, the party had nominated James Charles, George Charles' father, as its candidate for the Dennery-Micoud seat. However, John Compton had other ideas. He insisted on contesting the seat, so he entered and won the race as an independent candidate. This political move alienated John Compton from the party, but unrepentant he took up writing a column coined the "Jack Spaniard" in the *Workers Clarion*, a Union newspaper in which, according to George Charles, he denounced "the aristocracy and social discrimination."[6]

Compton was not one to stay out of the action for long. As alluded to earlier, during the famous 1957 sugar workers' strike, as a union activist and elected representative he entered the compound of the Dennery sugar factory to articulate the Union's demands, only to stare at the end of a gun held by Dennis Barnard, the grandfather of Dr. Kenny Anthony and the owner of the factory, and having to draw his own gun to bring the confrontation to a stalemate. This image, this symbol, of John Compton as the man who, like David facing Goliath, had single-handedly faced the enemy of the people, the enemy who had enslaved their ancestors, and returned unscathed and victorious, would further contribute to his mythical and epic-hero persona. According to George Charles, the strike heroics of Compton and others helped foster a feeling of brotherhood and camaraderie, thus the Labour Party warmly welcomed Compton back to the fold.[7]

The Labour Party won the 1961 general elections by a landslide of 9 seats, with the one remaining seat going to the People's Progressive Party (PPP). George Charles was appointed chief minister, but it would be a bittersweet victory because unfortunately for him, brotherhood or not, hero or not, personality tics do not just go away.

According to George Charles, disappointed that he was not made chief minister, John Compton (along with Maurice Mason and Vincent Monrose) withdrew his seat from the Labour government and defected to the PPP. Following which the PPP and the Compton faction brought a case to court that sought to nullify the results of the elections because the election supervisor had furnished the wrong form for candidate signatures. The Court ruled in favor of the petition, but the Administrator did not uphold the ruling. Having failed in their attempt to invalidate the elections and hence the government, the PPP and the Compton faction embarked on a series of public meetings to protest the administrator's refusal to abide by the court decision.

Compton, however, offered a different explanation for his defection. He said that with the 1961 general elections, "the complexion of the Labour Party started to change from the trade union base to more professional people," including John Compton himself, Dr. Vincent Monrose, Maurice Mason, and Clive Compton. Apparently, a chasm developed between the new breed of politicians, most of whom were college-educated or professionally trained, and the old guard who were less formally educated and who had emerged from the labor union movement. According to Compton, the old guard became suspicious of him and the other professionals, accusing them of seeking to take over the party, and referring to them as intellectuals, which was meant to be an insult. He said that the old guard, including George Charles, Martin 'Oleo' Jn Baptiste, and Herman Collymore, "gave us a hell of a time, so we found it intolerable, and we left."[8]

Which version to believe, John Compton's or George Charles'? Apparently, both. The old guard could not help but feel threatened by their younger, university-educated colleagues brimming with energy, passion, and ideas. On the other hand, John Compton, with his popularity, leadership ability, not to mention his personality tic, backed by a university degree, could not help but see himself as better able to head the government than George Charles who only had a secondary education.

Eventually, John Compton, along with Vincent Monrose and Maurice Mason, formed the National Labour Movement Party (NLMP). Then on April 1, 1964, the Bousquet brothers (J.M.D. and Allan Bousquet) resigned from the Labour Party, citing their dissatisfaction with the 1962 government restructuring of the SLBGA as the reason for their departure. With these defections and resignations, the Labour Party no longer had a majority in the house, so Chief Minister George Charles opted for a premature general election.

To contest this general election, the John Compton-led NLMP joined forces with the People's Progressive Party (PPP) to form the United Workers Party. At this 1964 general elections, the Labour Party won only two seats, while the United Workers Party, joined by the Bousquet brothers who had run and won as independent Labour candidates, carried eight seats. After the elections, the UWP elected John Compton as leader of the party, and John Compton replaced George Charles as chief minister of government.

Compton's personality tic of having to be the boss showed up soon after the UWP gained power. According to George Odlum,[9] John Compton was at loggerheads with Hunter Francios (a member of the PPP that joined forces with the NLMP to form the UWP), and as a result both men tendered their resignation from the party, so it was left to party chairman, Henry Giraudy, to step into the leadership role. But placing a high price on his independence and freedom, Giraudy had no such designs. Instead of taking up the mantle of leadership, he implored both men to return to the fold. Apparently, though they relented, the friction never completely dissipated. In 1974, a disenchanted Hunter Francois left the UWP to join the SLP.

George Odlum said that Giraudy declining the leadership role when it was his for the taking, made it clear to John Compton that no matter how powerful Giraudy became, he need not question his loyalty, he need not fear for his crown. In Giraudy, Compton had found a "political-comrade-in-arms." So apparently, Compton can work with competent and powerful persons once they are distant from political power, for example, civil servants; or it is clear they have (and will have) no designs on his throne. After all, he worked with an economic planning unit in the ministry of finance (which included Dwight Venner who would become the longtime governor of the Eastern Caribbean Central Bank and Ausbert D'Auvergne considered a guru in economic planning) that oversaw his transformation of the St. Lucian economy.

The Compton leadership tic showed up again in 2001 when, accusing the SLP government of playing a game of *bèlèlesh* (smoke and mirrors), George Odlum resigned from his post as foreign minister, and, not unlike 1982 when he had joined forces with John Compton to oust a discredited SLP government, Odlum again teamed up with the then retired John Compton to form a political alliance (not unlike the alliance Compton had forged back in 1964 between the NLMP and the PPP to form the UWP) with which they hoped to successfully contest the next general elections and then introduce a government of national unity.

In that alliance, a group of concerned citizens appointed George Odlum political leader, John Compton president, and Dr. Morella Joseph (leader of the UWP) vice president. However, just when the Alliance had gained national acceptance and momentum, and had become a serious threat to the Labour Party's rule come the 2001 election (and in the eyes of many, represented the country's only hope of removing Dr. Kenny Anthony and his Labour Party from power), a leadership struggle developed between George Odlum and John Compton. George Odlum accused John Compton of an unwillingness or inability to subordinate himself to anyone. And John Compton protested George Odlum's close ties with Libya's Muammar al-Qaddafi and the potential harm that could bring to St. Lucia.

At a National Alliance Assembly, which George Odlum chose not to attend, John Compton was unanimously elected political leader of the party. George Odlum denounced this new election as illegitimate and insisted that he was the political leader. Exasperated with the rivalry between the two men, and concluding that they were causing more harm than good, Dr. Morella Joseph divorced her United Workers Party from the Alliance and prepared her party for general elections. John Compton abandoned the Alliance and threw his support behind Dr. Morella Joseph and the UWP, leaving George Odlum to forge ahead with the much weaker and smaller National Alliance Party, of which he became the undisputed political leader. In this election, the Labour Party returned to power with a 14−3 majority

It may be fair to posit that it is this, John Compton's personality tic−an inability or unwillingness to work with persons well positioned or well equipped to challenge his leadership−as rightly pointed out by George Odlum, that is largely responsible for the seeming decline of the UWP and the emergence of Allen Chastanet as its leader.

To expound, the narrative begins with the 1993 banana no-cut strike since it is that event more than any other that marked the beginning of UWP's slide. As mentioned earlier, in 1993 farmers went on an island-wide banana no-cut strike that culminated in the shooting death of two farmers by police in the Mabouya Valley, in the district of Dennery. As if interpreting the strike and its aftermath as the "writing on the wall", Compton decided it was time, after nearly three decades, to give up the mantle of leadership. But apparently, unable to find anyone in his party he deemed worthy of filling his shoes, of continuing his legacy, he chose Dr. Vaughan Lewis, former secretary-general of the OECS, nephew of celebrated Nobel Laureate, Sir Arthur Lewis, and son of distinguished judge, and ex-governor general, Sir Allen Lewis. To hand Dr. Lewis the prime ministership, Compton requested of George Mallet, then UWP elected representative for Central Castries, to step down and allow Dr. Lewis to run for the seat in a by-election. Dr. Lewis won the race handsomely, and in mid-election term St. Lucians awoke to find a new prime minister running the country.

We have already seen how Vaughan Lewis at the helm of the UWP turned out—his party was beaten by the Kenny Anthony-led Labour Party in two consecutive landslide election victories; so much so, that watching his hard-earned legacy petering away, John Compton found it necessary to return to politics, wrestle the party leadership from Dr. Lewis, and then returned his party to glory in the 2006 general elections.

However, the fact that John Compton had to go outside his government to find a suitable replacement for the prime ministership, speaks to the personality tic mentioned above, which may be one of the greatest weaknesses of his legendary political career, and probably the biggest disfavor he may have done to his party and country.

As opposed to being groomed from within the party, Dr. Lewis was thrown into the political arena straight from academia or administration. There was no testing ground to ascertain that he had what it took to navigate the political waters and win elections. His failure at politics suggests that academics and intellect do not necessarily translate into effective political leadership and wherewithal to win elections. Charisma, eloquence, the ability to connect with people and to communicate in a manner that reaches persons of all backgrounds and levels of training and education are also part of the equation.

It appears that historically UWP has not been able to attract the caliber (in terms of education and training) of constituency candidates and other personnel that SLP has attracted, which may be partly a result of the Compton personality tic. The fact that in Choiseul-Saltibus, two doctors at the peak of their careers are fighting for the opportunity to represent the district under the SLP is not an aberration. It seems that from the time George Odlum and Peter Josie emerged on the political scene in the 1970s, the Labour Party has fielded more highly educated candidates than the UWP. SLP administrations are associated with a higher level of representation at all levels, from prime ministers, ministers, and senators, to ambassadors, to district constituency councils, to the persons who populate the Boards and Commissions of government agencies and statutory bodies.

Another ramification of the Compton tic is that it may have contributed to his untimely demise.

By the time Compton reentered politics to lead his party into the 2006 general elections, most of his UWP compatriots who probably shared his patriotism and vision for the country were deceased or retired from politics. A partial list includes Henry Giraudy, George Mallet, Allan Bousquet, Romanus Lansiquot, Ira D'Auvergne, Louis George, Clendon Mason, and Heraldine Rock.

The UWP inability to attract quality candidates who possess the ability to win their seats, and failure to groom such candidates from within, meant that Compton and UWP could not be choosers and may have welcomed candidates into their fold whom in days gone by Compton and Henry Giraudy would probably never have entertained. The result was that for the 2006 general elections Compton and UWP found themselves with a slate of candidates and district representatives of questionable character who may have been best characterized as opportunists rather than as patriots. Among them were suspected or convicted criminals, and Guy Joseph, the bus driver turned politician, who, as has been noted, seems to be at the center of every corruption charge leveled at Chastanet's UWP government.

This new crop of UWP politicians included the gang of eight ministers/district representatives who accosted and allegedly physically threatened John Compton in Cabinet in opposition to his reconsideration of the Taiwan – China diplomatic decision. Apparently, Compton had decided to continue diplomatic relations with China instead of switching to Taiwan as originally planned. A move that would have placed the gang of eight in a very awkward position if, as alleged, Taiwan had helped finance the party's campaign and had already given each of them a substantial bribe for their diplomatic allegiance.

The menacing confrontation must have come as an enormous shock to Compton, who throughout his political career reigned supreme over the UWP; and those who had a problem with that and could not stomach it were shown the door. But here he was, at the ripe age of 82, compelled to reenter politics to get his party back to power, facing a mutinous gang of questionable characters, and no Henry Giraudy in sight to impose some law and order. It was as if Compton suddenly realized that his new UWP parliamentary colleagues were a den of thieves, or worse, a pit of vipers. If so, is it any wonder that the same John Compton who had had the physical stamina and mental fortitude to make a four-hour marathon budget presentation, succumbed to illness and death shortly after the mutinous Cabinet confrontation?

As has been noted, after Compton's demise, the UWP turned into a dysfunctional government where every minister was a government unto himself, where Tom Chou, the Taiwanese Ambassador to St. Lucia, seemed to have more say in government than even the prime minister, where ministers were so readily in trouble with the law that one got the impression that the country was being ruled by a gang of criminals, where the US government was revoking ministers' diplomatic visas.

In this unfortunate state of affairs, Chastanet, who was minister of tourism, but was not an elected parliamentarian, and who was not part of the gang of eight and so was not tainted with Compton's blood, emerged as the minister that seemed most prime ministerial. Compared to his colleagues, he was articulate, proactive, and exuded confidence.

UWP lost the following 2011 elections, but Chastanet's bearing and performance in his stint as minister of tourism must have impressed the UWP. Of course, the party did not have too many great options to choose from for the leadership. They probably viewed Chastanet as the best among a basket of rotten mangoes. It has been shown how Chastanet grabbed the opportunity, pushing aside the usual suspects of Stephenson King, Lenard "Spider" Montoute, Richard Frederick, and Sarah Flood-Beaubrun to emerge as the leader of the party, and how he and his shaky UWP had defeated a tall-standing and over-confident Kenny Anthony-led Labour Party.

Back to how the UWP changed from the era of John Compton when it was regarded as the best government in St. Lucia's history to the era of Allen Chastanet being regarded as the worst.

Partly because of Compton's personality tic, the UWP apparently never had a succession plan and so failed to groom suitable leaders and also failed to consistently attract high caliber candidates. This deficiency led to a leadership and candidate crisis when John Compton stepped down and when his UWP contemporaries and those who immediately followed bowed out of politics. Out of this crisis of leadership and paucity of quality personnel, Chastanet emerged, not as a stellar candidate, but by default, as the candidate with the fewest negatives, as the best among an unimpressive bunch.

Part IV

The Need For Change

Rick Wayne, OBE
(born Learie Carasco, 27 January 1938)

World-renowned bodybuilder, and St. Lucia's most famous journalist. Regarded as a prime minister maker.

14

A POLITICAL
LEADERSHIP CRISIS

The SLP and UWP battle for national supremacy has many subplots, in fact as many subplots as there are electoral districts, for the battle is played out in each of the nation's 17 constituency districts, and it is the party that wins the most electoral seats that gets to govern.

The process by which the parties pick the candidate who will represent them in each electoral district and how representative or reflective is the selected candidate of the community's choice, and if elected how well will the candidate represent the best interest of the district, will all help determine the inclusiveness or extractiveness of the country's political system. Moreover, in the State of Urgency online poll, voters signaled that selecting competent people to be Cabinet ministers, which is a direct reflection of the quality of district reps (since most district reps are appointed ministers), is one of the most important considerations in changing for the better how government operates. Voters also believed that quality of (political) leadership was the second (only to unemployment) most critical issue facing the country.

The Choiseul-Saltibus Political Controversy

The Choiseul-Saltibus electoral district, situated at the southeast corner of the island, is home to the center of the island's folk craft industry and the descendants of its Amerindian population. In July 2020, the district was embroiled in a political subplot that may bode well for the country's political health.

The Labour Party apparatus nominated Dr. Pauline Prospere, an educator, as its candidate for the Choiseul-Saltibus seat, even after it appeared the district had clarified that their overwhelming choice was Dr. Alphonsus St. Rose, an internist and gastroenterologist, who, in a press release,[1] intimated that the "new realities" of "St. Lucia's (political) landscape" had compelled him to change his priority from "healthcare" to "the larger frontier of politics."

According to Dr. St. Rose, as evidenced in a "strongly worded petition of 700 signatures, most of the Labour supporters in the constituency have rejected the party's decision, which they rightly deem an assault on their freedom of choice and expression, fairness, due process, and justice." He characterized the party's candidate selection process as "tainted, rigged, manipulated, contaminated," and "mired in improprieties and irregularities."

Concerned that such infighting would undermine the party's chances of unseating the Chastanet regime, the SLP leadership invoked the Chastanet-must-go mantra and the Chastanet Ultimatum to persuade Dr. St. Rose and his supporters to fall in line.

For example, in addressing the controversy, Labour Party leader, Philip J. Pierre, wrote:

> It is important that we all do not lose sight of what is of paramount interest to the people of Saint Lucia at this time; and that is the removal of the inept and vindictive Allen Chastanet UWP Government from the backs of the Saint Lucian

people…It is imperative that we all unite to accomplish what is now our duty to ourselves and
our children.[2]

Dr. St. Rose and his followers did not take the bait. Instead,
the Chastanet Ultimatum backfired. The doctor said that although
they all wanted to see the Chastanet administration out of office,
"it would be wrong to swap it for a replacement that is equally
callous and intolerant of the views of the people." He reasoned
that "power resides in your vote which must define you better
than mere hostages for the removal of a candidate or a government
from office…we denounce any attempts to weaponize your vote
against you simply for expressing your constitutional right of
free choice."

Accordingly, in defiance of SLP leadership and riding the
wave of people power, Dr. St. Rose announced his decision to
bypass the Labour Party political machinery and contest the
Choiseul-Saltibus seat as an independent candidate. A decision
that represents the worst of all worlds for the Labour Party
because it is likely to split the Labour vote between the two
doctors, thus making it much more difficult for SLP to unseat
John Bradley Felix, the incumbent (UWP) district representative
and current minister for commerce, industry, investment, enterprise
development and consumer affairs.

However, the episode struck a blow for political empowerment
and inclusiveness, in that it emphasized that the political process,
including the selection of district representative candidates,
needs to be broad-based and an expression of the collective will
of the people, and not simply the dictate of a minority political
elite.

Moreover, the Labour Party should take this as an early
warning sign — do not sacrifice democracy, the will of the people,
and the formulation of a vision for the country for the expediency
of getting rid of Chastanet.

The Vieux Fort Political Leadership Crisis

For another take or subplot on electoral district politics, the narrative turns to the primary subject of this chapter, Vieux Fort's political leadership crisis.

Late 2019, I attended a SLP public meeting in Vieux Fort on Clarke Street, alongside Independence Square. It was a meeting of passionate, though repetitive, rhetoric. *SLP had had enough of Allen Chastanet's UWP government. UWP had to go!*

I waited with great anticipation for Dr. Kenny Anthony's address. When he came on, he was boisterous and forceful, as if what he had to say was a matter of life and death. He opened his salvo with: "Vieux Fortians are defiant." So the history buff that I am, particularly regarding the history of Vieux Fort, my hometown, I waited with bated breath for a trip down Vieux Fort's memory lane.

I expected to hear about the days when sugar was king, when to get a job in Vieux Fort's central sugar factory, one of the first of its kind in the Caribbean, one had to loan the overseer a sister, a daughter, or a niece. But rather than prostituting their womenfolk, in defiance, Vieux Fort men took to sea.[3]

I thought I would be told that the long-held view that Vieux Fortians are lazy is a myth, for if Vieux Fortians are lazy how then so many are fishermen when few occupations are as dangerous, harsh, and as demanding. Growing up, I thought the only occupation more dangerous than that of a fisherman was that of a soldier. That what some construe as the laziness and rudeness of Vieux Fortians are just Vieux Fortians' defiance and wariness of exploitation.

That, according to social historian, Dr. Jolien Harmsen,[4] Vieux Fort's hustler mentality of waiting for opportunities to come their way to quickly exploit and then wait again for the next opportunity, the next decider of their fate, is just a conditional response (a defiance mechanism of sorts) to history, to the fact that most of the happenings and developments that have transformed the district and changed its landscape have been dictated by outsiders, with Vieux Fortians having little or no say (DSH, the latest case in point), so Vieux Fortians have developed a wait and see attitude.

I thought the district rep would praise the likes of Julius James, Stephen Marcellin, Cynthia Satney, Raye Maxwell, Monty Maxwell, Cornelia Jacob and the other members of the Vieux Fort Concerned Citizens Coalition for Change (VFCCCC) for their defiance in building and holding the fort against Chastanet's DSH misadventure in Vieux Fort, when, smarting and still licking wounds from the 2016 electoral defeat, Labour politicians could barely hold their heads up, much less provide resistance to (what time may well prove to be) the Teo Ah Khing/Allen Chastanet ill-fated DSH development.

So imagine my disappointment, dismay, even, when Dr. Anthony explained with lots of conviction that Vieux Fortians are defiant because they refuse to vote UWP.

I said to myself, *this is the opposite of defiance. You mean no matter what you do, what you don't do, like doormats, Vieux Fortians continue voting for you?*

The Kenny Anthony Story Has Already Been Told

I reasoned the fact the former prime minister could so boldly and so confidently tell Vieux Fortians in effect they are not much better than doormats, and no one raised any objections, no one in the Labour Party seemed prepared to provide the district rep any opposition; and the fact of such blind loyalty, such thoughtless following, suggests that Vieux Fort is facing a political leadership crisis. I also reasoned that the emptiness of Dr. Anthony's speech, disguised in loudness and bluster, like a person increasing the volume of his speech to convince himself of its validity, suggests he was spent. Whatever he had to offer has been offered. His performance on that evening serving as a metaphor for what he had left to offer as a political representative.

I can never forget what the professor of the only creative writing college class (at Washington University, St. Louis, Missouri) I have taken said to us. He said that everyone has but one story in them; they may write many books, many novels, many poems, but each is just another take of the same story. Well, it seems Vieux Fortians have already read at least five takes of the Kenny Anthony story. Why read a sixth take? Aren't there any other interesting books waiting to be read? Won't it be more stimulating, more engaging, more fruitful to read the first take of another Vieux Fort district rep, this time one from the town and dedicated to its cause? Or is one saying Vieux Fortians are so deficient that a sixth reading of Kenny's story is more rewarding than the first reading of the story of the most exciting Vieux Fortian? Clearly, Vieux Fort needs to take a page from Dr. St. Rose and the district of Choiseul-Saltibus and show Kenny Anthony and the Labour Party the true meaning of defiance.

Vieux Fort a Political Playground

Too often politicians vie for the Vieux Fort seat, not because they are from Vieux Fort, not because they are passionate about Vieux Fort, not because they have a burning desire to develop Vieux Fort, but because of convenience. They see it as a safe seat, a seat to nurture their ambition, a seat from which to launch their national political career. It appears Vieux Fort is just a political playground (and Chastanet with his DSH has added that it is also a rich man's hunting ground), not a place with actual people with actual needs. All this reinforces the notion that Vieux Fort is facing a political leadership crisis.

Those who have won the Vieux Fort seat have either been non-Vieux Fortians, or lacked dedication to Vieux Fort, or did not have sufficient clout in government to do much for the district.

In reference to Table 2, take a look at the Vieux Fort political landscape beginning with the 1964 general elections that marked the entrance of the UWP onto the political stage and that ushered in statehood (1967). That year the UWP was voted into power, and Henry Giraudy won the Vieux Fort-Laborie seat. He won the seat again (Vieux Fort South) in 1974 in an election made famous by "It'll be all right in the morning" (the election officer's comforting words to a seemingly losing Henry Giraudy) and Rick Wayne's book[6] of the same title.

Henry Giraudy was born and raised in Vieux Fort, and he was UWP's long-serving and undisputed party chairman. Some say he was the power behind the John Compton throne. He had plenty of clout in the UWP and in government, but according to many Vieux Fortians he was a pompous, arrogant politician who thought Vieux Fortians beneath him and who was mainly concerned with national politics, with ensuring his party wins general elections and stays in power. Many can recall Giraudy at UWP public meetings shouting: "shut up and listen to your masters"; or he will *put his foot on his political opponents and crush them like crabs.* Come to think of it, is this any more arrogant and conceited than Kenny Anthony telling Vieux Fortians in effect they are defiant because they are doormats, because no matter what he does they will never stop voting for him and his Labour Party?

Bruce Williams, Vieux Fort's great humanitarian, affectionately known as Daddy Bruce because of his generosity and love of children, won the Vieux Fort-Laborie seat in 1969 on the SLP ticket, but in this general elections UWP had held on to power. Daddy Bruce won the Vieux Fort seat again in 1979, in the election that ended SLP's 15-year political drought, but SLP's reign, which turned into a debacle, was aborted in mid-term, a phenomenon aptly captured in *Foolish Virgins*,[7] the second book

Table 2.

Vieux Fort District Reps Since Universal Suffrage[5]

Election Year	Electoral District	Wining Candidate	Political Party
1951	Laborie – Vieux Fort	Antoine L. Theodore	PPP
1954	Laborie – Vieux Fort	Clive A. Marie Compton	SLP
1957	Laborie – Vieux Fort	Clive A. Marie Compton	SLP
1961	Vieux-Fort/Laborie	Clive A. Marie Compton	SLP
1964	Vieux-Fort/Laborie	Henry E. Giraudy	UWP
1969	Vieux-Fort/Laborie	Bruce W. Williams	SLP
1974	Vieux-Fort South	Henry E. Giraudy	UWP
1979	Vieux-Fort South	Bruce W. Williams	SLP
1982	Vieux-Fort South	Eldridge Stephens	UWP
1987	Vieux-Fort South	Peter Josie	SLP
1992	Vieux-Fort South	Peter Josie	SLP
1997	Vieux Fort South	Kenny D. Anthony	SLP
2001	Vieux Fort South	Kenny D. Anthony	SLP
2006	Vieux Fort South	Kenny D. Anthony	SLP
2011	Vieux Fort South	Kenny D. Anthony	SLP
2016	Vieux Fort South	Kenny D. Anthony	SLP

of Rick Wayne's political trilogy. Few if any could have questioned Bruce Williams' dedication and commitment to Vieux Fort. He spent years seeking reparation from the Americans/British for their World War II occupation of Vieux Fort. But during his political life his party was rarely in power and it was not clear how much clout he had in the SLP setup.

Eldridge Stephens, a bona fide Vieux Fortian, won the 1982 Vieux Fort seat under the UWP ticket. There is no reason to doubt his love of and commitment to Vieux Fort, but the fact that he was not made a minister of government may suggest that he did not have much clout in the UWP. If so, then one could conclude that he was not advantageously positioned to effect significant change in Vieux Fort.

Peter Josie won the Vieux Fort seat in 1987 and then again in 1992, both times under SLP. As a Labour district rep serving under a UWP administration, he was not advantageously positioned to help Vieux Fort progress. Josie claims he was raised in Vieux Fort, or at least spent some of his childhood in Vieux Fort. Nonetheless, whether or not he can be considered a Vieux Fortian, time has proven him to be an opportunist. In the middle of his second term as Vieux Fort district rep, he crossed the floor to the UWP camp to become a minister of government. Since then he has not looked back. It is amazing that the once socialist radical willing to face death marching and protesting with George Odlum and the agricultural workers in the nation's great valleys, and who during the 1979 election season used to shout on SLP political platforms across the nation something to the effect that *if we can't get in power by law, we will get in power by violence*, has become, some say, Rick Wayne's side-kick and has had nothing but praise for the UWP and Chastanet as (established in Part III) they seem to give away St. Lucia's sovereignty and patrimony to foreigners, as they seem to give away Vieux Fort—Josie's self-admitted hometown—to Chinese nationals, as they seem to extract income and resources from the masses for the benefit of family, friends and foreigners, and as they seem to undermine and corrupt the institutions and statutory bodies that were established to safeguard the integrity of the country and protect it against the greed and misadventures of politicians. As an opportunist one can conclude that Josie vying for the Vieux Fort seat was probably more about reviving and keeping his political career alive than about a commitment and dedication to Vieux Fort.

And then there is Dr. Kenny Anthony, three-time prime minister, district rep of Vieux Fort for five-terms, spanning 24 years, from 1997 to 2021, and still counting.

Following the 1993 banana fiasco that culminated in the shooting death of two banana farmers in the Mabouya Valley,

one of three of St. Lucia's great agricultural valleys, Labour
Party stalwarts paved the way (rolled the red carpet, even) for
Dr. Anthony to leave the comfort of the CARICOM Secretariat in
Guyana and come wrestle the island from the stranglehold of
John Compton and the UWP and lead the Labour Party to
electoral victory. Part of that paved road was to assign Kenny
Anthony to Vieux Fort, a safe Labour seat, thus ensuring his
prime ministership were Labour to claim national victory.

How safe? Well, in St. Lucia's 70 years, 16 general elections,
of universal suffrage, Labour has lost only four Vieux Fort elections — 1951 to Antoine Theodore of the People's Progressive
Party (Vieux Fort-Laborie seat), 1964 and 1974 to Henry Giraudy
(UWP) and 1982 to Eldridge Stephens (UWP). Kenny Anthony's
five terms make him the longest-standing Vieux Fort district rep
ever, the next closest being Clive Compton (Vieux Fort-Laborie
seat) who as the SLP candidate won three terms (1954, 1957,1961),
coinciding with three of the first four elections held under
universal suffrage.

Kenny Anthony is not from Vieux Fort (though he attended
secondary school there), and right from the start his representation
of Vieux Fort had little to do with passion and dedication to the
district, definitely not the passion exhibited by Dr. St. Rose in his
defiance of the Labour Party, but all to do with a safe perch from
which to launch his national political career, in the process
bringing Sir John's political dynasty to an end.

Did Kenny Anthony Ever Have a Vision for Vieux Fort?

Some Vieux Fortians believe that Kenny Anthony never had a
vision for Vieux Fort. He inherited from John Compton projects
in planning, some of which he implemented — the fishery complex,
for example — but mostly his involvement in Vieux Fort has been
more about appeasing Vieux Fortians to continue securing their

vote (what he calls defiance) than about substance, job creation, social and economic transformation. As an example, some point out that while the district rep built footpaths, repaved sidewalks, paved a so-called promenade, opened up what used to be called the Mangue, and renovated the Vieux Fort Square, he had failed to secure three million US dollars for a new crane that would have helped maintain the viability and vitality of Port Vieux Fort, a significant source of Vieux Fort employment.

Notwithstanding, it does not mean that Dr. Anthony is not deserving of some praise. As suggested in Chapter 6, he inculcated a greater level of professionalism in government and governance, fostered a kinder and gentler nation, and ushered St. Lucia into the twenty-first century.

To this some would argue, fine, but most of this was accomplished by the end of Kenny Anthony's first term. So at most he should have been given just two terms. After two terms his story was already fully written, beyond two terms was just a recycle of the story. He was spent. It was a mistake to have changed the Labour Party constitution to allow him to run a third term as party leader, reminiscent of when George Odlum had orchestrated a change in St. Lucia's constitution to allow him to become a minister of government in the 1979 SLP administration. St. Lucia may have been better served to have allowed Mario Michel, the next in line to the throne, the opportunity to write his story across the St. Lucia political landscape.

Come to think of it, what hold does Kenny Anthony has on St. Lucia and the Labour Party that they keep changing constitutions to accommodate his political career? Is it the same hold (defiance he calls it) he has on Vieux Fort that the district keeps voting for him no matter what?

Back in 1997 when Labour won the elections by a 16 to 1 landslide, and then again in 2001 by 14 to 3, Vieux Fortians were probably ecstatic, for who better able to bring home the bacon than the prime minister who doubles as one's district rep. After all, they had rolled the red carpet for Dr. Anthony, given him their loyalty, which he calls defiance, in spades. Vieux Fortians, that is those old enough to remember the "Time of the Americans,"[8] or those paying attention to their history, were probably in smiles, thinking the good times will roll again. And who could blame them? Does not the good book say (Luke 12:48): "*For unto whomsoever much is given, of him shall be much required: and to whom men have committed much, of him they will ask the more.*"

If Kenny Anthony should have done no more than two terms as prime minister of St. Lucia, then five terms as Vieux Fort district rep were more than enough, particularly since no one seems to be accusing him of setting ablaze the social and economic development of Vieux Fort. Now, it made sense for Vieux Fort to suffer Kenny Anthony as district rep as long as he was party leader, because as mentioned above the best of all worlds is for the prime minister to double as one's district rep. But since he is no longer party leader and thus has no chance of becoming prime minister, there is little gain in having him as the district rep as opposed to a qualified, bona fide Vieux Fortian. Besides, apparently, once Kenny Anthony is not occupying the prime minister's seat he goes missing in action. Still, if he were to Vieux Fort what Alva Baptiste was to Laborie or what Moses "Musa" Jn Baptiste was to Vieux Fort North—two ideal models of a district rep—Vieux Fortian or not, prime minister or not, Vieux Fort could have borne with him. But an Alva or a Moses he is not.

And in terms of economic well-being, Vieux Fort does not have much to shout about. In 2016 the district registered a poverty rate of 34.6 percent (percentage of the population who are poor), an increase of 11.5 percentage points from the 23.1 percent recorded in 2006. This meant that Vieux Fort was the third poorest, behind Anse La Raye/Canaries and Dennery, of St. Lucia's 10 districts.[9] In terms of joblessness, Vieux Fort suffers from the highest unemployment rate of all districts. Its 2019 unemployment rate of 32.4 percent was 12 to 16 percentage points above the national average. For eight of the past ten years (2010-2019), its unemployment rate exceeded that of all districts, such that its average annual unemployment rate of 34.5 was 8 percentage points higher than that of Dennery with the second highest rate.[10]

Yet, with an international airport making it the gateway of St. Lucia, a seaport accommodating ocean-going vessels, the largest expanse of flat land of any district, a wealth of American bequeathed road infrastructure, complexes of ready-made factory/plant shells, rich fishing waters that have made it the fishing capital of the country, a milieu of unique natural, historical, and cultural attractions including the island's longest and most inviting stretch of white sandy beach, and a pleasant and healthy climate of salt-laden, air-conditioning Trade-winds, Vieux Fort has plenty going for it. Therefore, what excuse can one give for Vieux Fort occupying the bottom rank of St. Lucia's economic health?

Vieux Fortians' view of Kenny Anthony isn't monolithic. While some are saying "Kenny Anthony didn't do anything for Vieux Fort", at least one Vieux Fortian has expressed a slightly different point of view. He opined that he isn't one to focus too much on what Kenny Anthony did or didn't do for Vieux Fort, because a prime minister has to address the development needs of the entire country, and not just his district. As such, there is competition among district reps for resources for their districts, so no matter how much a prime minister cares about his district, there is a limit on how much he can do for it. However, where he faulted Kenny Anthony was his approach to overseeing Vieux Fort. In Vieux Fort, Kenny Anthony had access to a cadre of educated and capable Labour supporters, dedicated to and passionate about Vieux Fort, who even actively campaigned for him and the Labour Party. Kenny Anthony could have leverage himself through these persons by letting them guide him and help him identify and prioritize the development imperatives of Vieux Fort and then seek to systematically fulfill these imperatives. But as soon Kenny Anthony won the elections, he more or less ostracized this cadre of Vieux Fort patriots, and instead courted party hacks with much less to offer and with little demonstrated dedication to Vieux Fort, whose main qualifications were unquestionable loyalty to Kenny Anthony and a willingness to keep him informed of what other SLP members were saying about him. It is in this way that he felt the Vieux Fort South district rep and former prime minister had failed his constituency.

Of course, Kenny Anthony may respond with the fact that his government had fostered the establishment of the Southern Tourism Development Cooperation (STDC), which with a government subvention was charged with overseeing and spearheading tourism development in Vieux Fort and the southern half of the island. So empowered, the STDC could have easily broadened its scope to general economic and social development. In other words, STDC could have viewed itself as the entity running Vieux Fort.

Nonetheless, many Vieux Fortians were totally flabbergasted that, given Kenny Anthony's lack of political involvement following the 2016 elections, leaving the challenge to Teo Ah Khing and Chastanet's DSH to his surrogates in the VFCCCC, and also given that Vieux Fort was not jumping for joy from economic upliftment, he was running again for the Vieux Fort South seat. They could be forgiven to have thought Kenny Anthony had finished with electoral politics. To some, their astonishment turned to anger. *When is Kenny going to have enough and give a Vieux Fortian a chance?*

From the days of slavery and when sugar was king, to the time of the Americans during World War II, to the days when banana was king, to the days of Halcyon Days, industrialization, and the "last frontier", and now to the days of DSH and Teo Ah Khing, Vieux Fort has always been led by outsiders, strangers have always decided its fate. Now it is a time for change, now it is a time for Vieux Fortians to lead themselves, to borrow a page from the Choiseul-Saltibus electoral district and take their future into their own hands, to be led by a district rep who is from the people, of the people, and has demonstrated an unsurpassed dedication, passion and commitment to the cause of Vieux Fort. A leader is needed who, when it comes to Vieux Fort, will not take no for an answer; someone who will never sell Vieux Fort out: not for money, not for Teo Ah Khing's fancy development designs and membership into his Shanghi Race Club, not for foreigners, not for Miami Beach, not for national or international fame, not for privilege, not for favors.

When one grows up breathing in the salt-laden breeze of Vieux Fort's Atlantic coast; loitering among the sea grape, fat poke, and almond trees, feasting on their fruit; frolicking on the various beaches that surround Vieux Fort with names like Sandy, Bwa Chadon, L'anse Baison, and New Dock; marveling at the wide-open spaces; trekking Moule-a-Chique to the lighthouse; playing ball on Vieux Fort's Savannes; jogging across the Vieux Fort landscape; racing horses on the Kaka Bef; diving off the Dock and the Jetty; and fishing on the Dock and other strategic fishing spots, one can never see Vieux Fort as an empty wilderness perfect for fulfilling one's political career or realizing one's ambition of a Miami Beach/Dubai Palm Islands or as real estate gifts to foreigners for club membership. How could one, when the place is part of one's self-definition, when the place and its people are in one's blood? Instead, like Julius James and some other members of the VFCCCC, one gets up each morning ready to battle for the upliftment and progress of one's town, sharpening one's weapons to defend it against foreign and misguided adventurers. Shouldn't it be that the people who care the most about a place and would be the most affected by any changes to it, be the ones who should have the most say in what happens to the place, the ones to take the lead in its development?

What probably bothers Vieux Fortians the most is that strangers — be it Invest St. Lucia, or the Castries-based government, or the Americans, or the British, or the Chinese — invade their home, change it however they please, and no amount of cursing, no amount of vexation, no amount of anguish, no amount of protest, can change that.

A Vieux Fortian characterized the DSH misadventure best.

> A man invites himself to your home, expels you from your house and land, takes your woman and daughters as wives, and builds a hotel on your land. Now destitute and landless and fami-ly-less you have little choice but to come begging the man for a job taking care of the hotel grounds. Looking down at you with contempt, the man grudgingly gives you the job, causing you and the whole nation to celebrate the job creation magic of hotels.

There is a crop of potential candidates who come to mind that may fit the bill — Julius James, Monty Maxwell, Augustus Cadette, Cynthia Satney, the former senator, Debra Tobierre, and I'm sure there are others.

But there is a problem. Under Kenny Anthony, the Labour Party has adopted a culture of strict party discipline and loyalty, a culture of everyone toeing the line, even when, as with the recent Choiseul-Saltibus SLP candidate selection, the party's de-cision is contrary to the will of the people. Of course, Kenny An-thony calls it by another name — defiance. Moreover, it seems the party has placed Kenny Anthony on a pedestal. No one dares to cross him, much less challenge his leadership, much less present themselves as an alternative SLP choice for the Vieux Fort seat. And no aspiring SLP Vieux Fort candidate dares to go the route of Dr. St. Rose and join the race as an independent candidate. Therefore, unless Kenny Anthony steps down and gives the green light to the next would be SLP candidate, Vieux Fort will not get a change, the district will be stuck with him, Vieux Fortians will have to read yet another take of his story.

15

PERSISTENT UNEMPLOYMENT

In Chapter 1, it was mentioned that SLP seems to be of the view that the biggest problem facing St. Lucia is Allen Chastanet, that the country's problems begin and end with him, and that getting rid of his UWP government would return the country to the good times. So much so that SLP is threatening voters with the Chastanet Ultimatum—*Vote Labour or suffer the Allen Chastanet train wreck.*

So then let us see whether the State of Urgency online poll can throw some light on SLP's predisposition. The poll showed that only 16 percent of respondents were satisfied with the way the UWP government was running the country, but an equally low percentage were satisfied with the way the SLP opposition was doing its job. Regarding dissatisfaction, SLP fared better; 61 percent of respondents were dissatisfied with the way the government was running the country, while 49 percent were dissatisfied with the way the opposition was doing its job. The poll results rated SLP more highly than UWP in managing the country when it is in power. For example, UWP highest approval scores were 20 and 18 percent compared to SLP highest scores of 36 and

31 percent. And UWP lowest approval scores were 5 and 8 percent compared to SLP lowest scores of 12 and 12.5 percent. These results suggest that SLP has the edge over UWP in terms of voter approval, but they do not suggest a clear endorsement of SLP. Therefore, the extent to which voters are fearful of the Chastanet Ultimatum and are buying into the notion that Chastanet-must-go is debatable.

What is clear, however, is that respondents cited unemployment as the most critical issue facing the country, further emphasizing that voters may not share the SLP sentiment that Chastanet is the biggest or most urgent problem the country faces.

This chapter therefore turns to the vexing problem of St. Lucia's persistently high unemployment that is gnawing at the social fabric of the country and which the State of Urgency poll respondents believe is one of the biggest problems the nation has to grapple with.

However, if one listens to politicians on both sides of the isle, one would be tempted to think unemployment is just a campaign issue, a fleeting phenomenon, one that only needs addressing at the time of elections. Yet, as mentioned in Chapter 9, *Putting St. Lucians First*, with a perennial unemployment rate of 15 to 25 percent and a youth unemployment rate of over 30 percent, the country is in a permanent Great Recession or, worse, a permanent Great Depression.

The 2011 election campaign may stick in one's mind because, more than any other campaign one may recall, it focused on alleviating the country's unemployment woes. The proposed unemployment busting measures were bold and bombastic. Besides an injection of $100 million into the economy, Dr. Kenny Anthony, then leader of the opposition Labour Party, proposed a host of unemployment busting measures and programs,[1] including the reintroduction of STEP but with a skills training component; employment tax incentives to businesses; and the creation of such entities as LEAP (an unemployment fighting unit), Office of Reconstruction (a road infrastructure reconstruction unit), and a National Job Placement Center. A would-be Labour government also planned to introduce such programs as Elderly Home Help to generate employment among single mothers, a Land Bank Program to engage young persons to work in high value-added agriculture, and a Business Grants Program to enable businesses to provide job skills training to secondary school students.

Finally, according to Dr. Anthony, a Labour government would increase the availability of technical and vocational training in secondary schools, provide greater support to the Junior Achievement Program and the St. Lucia Youth Business Trust, and overhaul and restructure the country's investment regime and institutions, including the National Development Corporation (NDC), to induce greater inflows of foreign investment.

Not to be outdone, in an interview with the St. Lucia Star Newspaper, the then prime minister, Stephenson King, said that while on a fact-finding tour of the country's economically depressed communities, it suddenly dawned on him, "like an epiphany," that the solution to the country's unemployment problem is to provide deserving businesses with financial incentive packages geared toward stimulating employment. The prime minister proposed a $300 million employment stimulus package to businesses.[2]

The Kenny Anthony-led Labour Party won the 2011 elections, and as noted in Chapter 9, *Putting St. Lucians Last*, the government implemented many of the employment measures advocated on the campaign trail, which altogether may represent the most comprehensive employment initiative package ever undertaken by an administration. The suggestion is not that these programs are not effective in creating employment, because obviously they do. For example, in 2014 Kenny Anthony revealed that NICE had benefited nearly 5000 persons and employed about 1100 workers.[3] However, it is not clear that governments fully appreciate the gravity, persistency, and permanency of the unemployment situation. They seem to view the problem as one which recently emerged, and all what is required to cure it is a set of temporary measures, which do not get to the bottom of the problem. Sometimes one gets the impression that their employment proposals and attempts at reducing unemployment are more about appeasing the populace to win votes than about seriously addressing the country's unemployment predicament.

But unemployment should be the last thing to play political football with. Its economic and social consequences are well documented. Unemployment impoverishes the nation and its people because it means less output and less household income than otherwise. Unemployment can lead to family disintegration, poor health and nutrition, inadequate housing, detrimental lifestyle changes, and the neglect of education. It causes psychological damage in the form of low self-esteem, loss of self-worth and mental depression. Out of desperation, it engenders the unemployed to seek illegal and underground means of material survival and thus creates a climate of crime and lawlessness. Protracted unemployment among groups can relegate them to ghettos of underclass citizens where economic activity is largely underground, where there is a disconnect with the larger society, and where a sub-culture of desperation and antisocial behavior prevails that renders many underclass citizens unemployable, such that even when there is an abundance of employment opportunities they may be incapable of availing themselves of jobs.

The UN office for the coordination of humanitarian affairs (OCHA) is in agreement with this assessment. It noted that St. Lucia's high unemployment rates are "prompting 'brain-drain' and human capital deterioration, which in turn have led to social exclusion and vulnerability, as well as a growing at-risk youth population and increased levels of violent crime."[4]

Given the dire consequences of unemployment, it may be useful to begin a national dialog on the country's unemployment woes, seek to characterize and dissect the problem, and suggest how St. Lucia can move toward a full employment economy. Therefore, this chapter provides a definition of unemployment and how it is measured, highlights some salient features of the unemployment situation in St. Lucia, identifies the causes, and in broad strokes suggests how the country can approach the problem with the goal of achieving full employment.

Definition and Salient Features

The unemployment rate is the percentage of the labor force that is not only out of work but is seeking employment. The labor force is defined as the percentage of the population 15 years and over who are employed or are seeking employment.

To arrive at these measures, the department of statistics conducts a random survey of persons around the island. Respondents who said they are both out of work and seeking employment are counted as unemployed members of the labor force, while those who are jobless but have stopped looking for work are not considered part of the labor force and thus are not included among the unemployed.

In 2015 St. Lucia had an estimated population of 140,680 persons of age 15 or older. Of this population, 101,608 were in the labor force. Of the labor force, 77,131 were employed and 24,477 were unemployed. The unemployment rate thus stood at 24.1 percent. Another 5,555 persons were jobless but did not factor into the labor force and unemployment statistics because they were not seeking employment.[5]

The irony of these statistics is that since by discontinuing their job search people exit the labor force, they help to decrease the unemployment rate statistic. In an economic recession, the jobless are less optimistic about finding employment and thus are more likely to exit the labor force, causing the unemployment statistic to fall. Therefore, the unemployment rate, particularly in a recession, provides an underestimation of the true economic plight of the country.

To address this phenomenon, which is considered part of what is called hidden unemployment, and to account for the jobless non-job seekers, the statistics department computes what it calls a relaxed unemployment rate by adding to the unemployment rate the rate of jobless non-job seekers obtained by dividing the number of jobless non-job seekers by the labor force. Accordingly, the relaxed unemployment rate for 2015 was computed as 29.6 percent, which probably represented a more realistic view of the country's economic plight.

Hidden unemployment may also result from governments' manipulation of the statistics to make the economy look better than it is, something of which the SLP has been accusing the Chastanet government because of seemingly inexplicable drops in reported unemployment rates.

For highlights of some salient features of St. Lucia's unemployment, take a look at Table 3, which provides unemployment rates and real GDP growth rates for the 1991-2019 period.

GDP or Gross Domestic Product is the market value of all final goods and services produced within a country in a given period. GDP provides a measure of the size of an economy, and the GDP growth rate is a measure of the rate at which an economy is expanding. Real GDP is GDP adjusted or discounted for inflation (the rate at which an economy's general price level is rising). By discounting GDP for inflation, one arrives at a GDP measure that captures growth in actual economic activity and not growth resulting from changes in prices.

The unemployment rate and GDP growth rate are two of the most relied upon indicators of the health of an economy. The two indicators are not unrelated. As business activity increases and the economy expands, one can expect unemployment to fall as existing firms increase hiring and new firms enter the market

	GDP Growth[6]	Unemploy-ment[6]	Relaxed Unemploy-ment[7]	Youth Unemploy-ment[7]
Year				
1991	0.4	16.6		
1992	8.0	16.6		
1993	0.6	16.8		
1994	1.6	17.0		
1995	1.7	15.8		
1996	2.9	16.3		
1997	-0.7	20.5		
1998	6.3	21.6		
1999	2.7	18.1		
2000	0.0	16.5		
2001	-3.4	18.3		
2002	0.4	20.4		
2003	4.3	22.2		
2004	7.3	21.0		
2005	-0.4	18.7		
2006	6.2	16.0		
2007	1.7	14.0		
2008	4.9	12.7		
2009	-2.8	15.4		
2010	1.6	17.1		
2011	5.5	18.9	27.1	35.3
2012	-0.2	19.1	26.7	33.9
2013	-3.2	22.2	28.1	39.6
2014	1.8	23.2	29.6	41.8
2015	-1.4	24.1	29.6	41.0
2016	4.0	21.3	25.7	38.4
2017	3.5	21.1	23.8	38.5
2018	2.6	20.9	22.6	36.3
2019	1.7	20.7	20.1	31.6

Table 3.

St. Lucia GDP Growth and Unemployment Rates

to take advantage of opportunities presented by a growing economy.

One glaring feature of St. Lucia's economy that the table makes clear is that no matter the GDP growth rate, the unemployment rate almost never falls below 15 percent, and the relaxed unemployment rate almost never falls below 20 percent. In 1992 the economy grew by 8 percent, yet the accompanying unemployment rate of 16.6 percent was higher than the 15.8 percent registered in 1995 when the economy grew by only 1.7 percent. In 1998 the economy expanded by 6.3 percent but registered an unemployment rate of 21.6 percent, which was higher than the 18.3 percent observed in 2001 when the economy contracted by 3.4 percent. In 2011, despite a 5.5 percent rate of economic growth, unemployment stood at 18.9 percent and relaxed unemployment at 27.1 percent. Fast forwarding to more recent times, in 2016 the economy grew by 4 percent, experienced an unemployment rate of 21.3 percent and a relaxed unemployment rate of 25.7 percent, which were higher than the unemployment rate and relaxed unemployment rate of 2018 when the economy expanded by 2.6 percent.

Apparently, no matter the political party in power or the state of the economy as measured by growth in GDP, unemployment remains at unacceptable levels. Contrary to what political operatives may want the populace to believe, St. Lucia's persistently high unemployment rate can hardly be blamed on world economic downturns or on the government of the day. Maybe a world recession can explain an unemployment jump from say 19 to 24 percent, but how about the 19 percent that existed before the recession?

In the most recent global economic meltdown,[8] coined the Great Recession in the US, that some were comparing with the Great Depression, the worldwide economic downturn of the 1929 -1941 period that ravaged the world, there was never a month where the unemployment rate rose above 10.6 percent. In the Great Depression, US unemployment rose no higher than 25 percent. Yet in any given year no one is surprised when (as in 2015) St. Lucia's unemployment rate rises above 24 percent and its relaxed unemployment above 29 percent. The country has a problem of persistently high unemployment that does not seem to change much even when one introduces unemployment busting measures; a problem that is rarely discussed and apparently goes unnoticed until the coming of elections.

So then it behooves us to delve deeper into St. Lucia's stubbornly high unemployment predicament to identify its likely causes and arrive at plausible solutions.

Determinants

Natural disasters of which hurricanes are the primary culprit, the decline of the banana industry, and global economic downturns have been cited as major causes of St. Lucia's high unemployment rate.

Regarding bananas, the phasing out of preferential treatment for St. Lucia bananas on the European market in the 1990s and the accompanying trade policy uncertainty and decreases in export prices caused the banana industry to nosedive — events that, as discussed in previous chapters, sparked the 1993 islandwide banana strike that culminated in the police shooting death of two banana farmers and that precipitated the liberalization and transformation of the banana industry in St. Lucia. Banana exports declined from 123 thousand metric tons in 1993, representing 12 percent of GDP, to a low of 6.6 thousand metric tons in 2011, accounting for only 0.5 percent of GDP.[9,10,11] Clearly, given how important the industry was to the economy, one can expect such a substantial decline to have a negative impact on GDP and employment. However, the fall of the banana industry cannot explain the observed long-term unemployment rate, because even in 1992 when banana exports were at a near all-time peak of 135.3 thousand metric tons and the economy expanded by 8 percent, the unemployment rate was still at nearly 17 percent. Moreover, although the economy has adjusted to the contraction of the banana industry — some farmers switched to other crops, others took up employment overseas or in other domestic industries; and tourism and other sectors picked up some of the slack—as evidenced in the 2.7 percent annual GDP growth rate in the decade (1998-2008) following the start of the decline, the unemployment rate remains stubbornly high.

Hurricanes are perennial nemeses to the Caribbean islands, and the destruction they wreak can cause considerable distress and decline in production and employment, particularly in the agricultural sector. However, the agricultural sector recovers quickly from the debilitating effects of hurricanes, and thus the impact on employment is temporary. St. Lucia's high unemployment rate prevails in both the absence and presence of hurricanes.

As a small, open economy heavily dependent on tourism, St. Lucia is very susceptible to global economic downturns and accompanying cyclical unemployment. For example, the Great Recession (2007 - 2009) has been blamed for the country's economic difficulties during the 2009 - 2015 period when the economy experienced negative growth rates for 4 of the 7 years and registered a meager annual average growth rate of 0.2 percent (Table 3). During that period, the economy also suffered a rise in unemployment from 15.4 percent to a peak of 24.1 percent. Like with hurricanes and the banana industry, global economic downturns cannot explain St. Lucia's perennially high unemployment, which remains elevated even when the economy is in an expansionary phase. Therefore, hurricanes, the decline of the banana industry, and global economic shocks account for temporary or occasional upswings in unemployment and thus help explain the fluctuation of the unemployment rate around an apparent long-run trend of 18 to 19 percent, but they do not explain the trend itself.

Besides cyclical unemployment, other types of unemployment include seasonal, frictional, and structural unemployment. Workers face frictional unemployment when they are in-between jobs, meaning they are searching for jobs or have left their old jobs and are moving to new jobs. Seasonal unemployment refers to discernable patterns of unemployment fluctuation over the course of the year. Structural unemployment can occur when workers are unable or unwilling to avail themselves of jobs as for example when they cannot relocate or commute to where jobs are available, or when they refuse to accept jobs because of a mismatch between the wage rate and their reservation wage. Structural unemployment can also occur when there is a mismatch between requisite job skills and the skills workers possess; and between the wage rate and the productivity or marginal revenue product of workers. When any of these mismatches occur, employment will be lower than otherwise.

Structural Unemployment

Unlike frictional and cyclical unemployment, structural unemployment tends to be long-term and slow to reverse, thus St. Lucia's persistently high unemployment may be best explained by structural unemployment. And as alluded to above, seasonal, frictional, and cyclical unemployment explain unemployment fluctuations around the long-run unemployment trend, but not the trend itself.

Reservation Wage

The reservation wage is the lowest wage for which a worker would be willing to accept a particular type of job. Workers who refuse to accept jobs at prevailing market wages (which are below their reservation wage) will remain unemployed thus adding to structural unemployment. The higher the reservation wage the greater the structural unemployment. Research has shown that remittances and high paying tourism and public sector jobs can cause high reservation wages, which, particularly when out of line with the marginal product of labor (production gained from an additional unit of labor), can help explain high structural unemployment.[12] High paying tourism and public sector jobs have positive impacts on reservation wages because workers come to view the wages of these sectors as the wage or employment standard by which to compare other jobs and to which they should aspire, anything less being tantamount to selling themselves short.

Remittance income is another factor that can have a positive impact on reservation wages because by helping to reduce the financial despair or needs of recipient households, it allows them to be more selective in the jobs and wages they accept. The Caribbean has a large diaspora, so one can expect the region to be the recipient of substantial amounts of remittances.

Kim has shown that Jamaican households receiving remittance income have higher reservation wages and are less likely to take up employment, and this helps explain the country's high structural unemployment and the anomaly that its real wages (wages adjusted for inflation) keep rising in the face of high unemployment.[13]

In 2016 remittances accounted for 17 percent of Jamaica's GDP compared to only about 2 percent of St. Lucia's, thus the impact of remittances on St. Lucia's reservation wage is unlikely to be as pronounced as Jamaica's.[12] However one can expect remittances to put upward pressure on St. Lucia's reservation wages and thus on its structural unemployment.

In 2013, the average salary of St. Lucia's tourism industry was 50 percent higher than that of formal agriculture. Similarly, public sector salaries were 63 percent higher. This wage disparity between tourism/public sector jobs and jobs of other sectors, has not only exacerbated the rural-urban drift but has raised the reservation wages of all workers in households with persons employed in tourism and the public sector. With higher reservation wages, these workers are more likely than others to abstain from jobs they deem too strenuous or beneath their status.[12]

Skills Mismatch

St. Lucian businesses often complain that they have difficulty securing workers with the specific skills their jobs require, which implies that the supply of workers with requisite job skills is insufficient to meet demand. This mismatch or deficiency has been cited as a possible cause of high structural unemployment because firms may be hiring fewer workers than they would have if the circumstances were different. However, the evidence of this disparity for St. Lucia is mixed. A 2012 national labor market needs survey revealed that whereas 60 percent of job seekers had less than secondary level of education, 75 percent of job vacancies required secondary education or above. And while 40 percent of job offers were made to candidates with tertiary education, only 7 percent of job seekers were similarly educated. The survey thus suggests a mismatch between the qualifications of job seekers and the requirements of job openings.[12]

But other evidence suggests that this may not be a binding constraint on the job market, and even if it were its impact on unemployment would be slight. For example, according to James et al.[12] the number of job vacancies requiring tertiary education (357) is far less than job seekers with tertiary education (1547), and filling all job vacancies requiring tertiary education would only reduce the unemployment rate by 0.37 percentage points.

It would appear St. Lucia has such a relatively vast pool of job seekers, that businesses are likely to find suitable candidates for most job openings, thus the job skill mismatch would only become a binding constraint as the economy moves toward full employment, which would be good news for the country.

Wage-Productivity Mismatch

Economic theory suggests that businesses follow the employment rule of hiring workers up to the level of output or economic activity where the marginal cost of labor (MCL) is just equal to the marginal revenue product of labor (MRPL). The MCL, which is usually the wage rate, is the addition to total cost of hiring an extra worker. The MRPL is the additional revenue a business generates from employing an additional worker and is obtained from multiplying the marginal product of labor (MPL) by the product price. The MPL is the addition to output obtained from hiring an additional worker and provides an indication of a worker's productivity. According to this employment rule, all else equal, the lower the wage rate and or the greater the MPL or the productivity of labor, the more workers businesses will employ and the greater their output or economic activity. The employment rule makes intuitive business sense because given that the firm is in business to maximize profits it would only hire an extra worker if the gain in revenues is greater or equal to the cost of the additional hire.

This brings to mind my favorite of the gospels of Dr. Payne, my intermediate microeconomic theory professor at Louisiana State University. "If you are in a job and what you are adding to the firm is less than what you are being paid, then it is time to look for another job because you won't have that job for much longer."

This economic theory digression is to point out that when wages are artificially high, meaning they are not in keeping with the marginal product of labor or the productivity of workers, businesses will find it unprofitable to hire their full quota of workers and thus will employ fewer workers than otherwise. Therefore, mismatches between the wage rate and the productivity of labor or MPL can lead to persistently high structural unemployment.

The evidence seems to support the notion that the wage level in St. Lucia is artificially high. According to a World Bank study,[14] even when productivity differences are accounted for, compared to other upper-middle-income countries, average wages in the Eastern Caribbean Currency Union (ECCU) were 25 percent higher for unskilled and semiskilled workers and 45 percent higher for professionals. Another study found that ECCU unit labor cost in the tourism sector was significantly higher than those of competing neighboring countries as the Bahamas, Dominican Republic, and Mexico.[12]

The unit labor cost (ULC) measures the average cost of labor per unit of output and indicates how much a business has to compensate (wages and benefits) workers to produce a unit of output. Thus the higher the ULC the fewer workers firms will employ. The ULC is closely related to the employment rule discussed above, and it is used to compare the competitiveness of countries or economic sectors. The competitiveness of a country or economic sector is inversely related to the ULC. An increase in compensation would cause ULC to rise, while an increase in labor productivity would cause it to fall. A wage rate is artificially high when it cannot be justified based on labor productivity, which implies that the best way to engender a pay raise is to become more useful, more productive to one's employer. Artificially high wages distort the labor market, lead to suboptimal levels of employment and production, and serve as disincentives to labor productivity.

Other results of the previously mentioned study established a positive and significant relationship between labor cost and unemployment and suggest that a 10 percent rise in unit labor cost was likely to cause a 3.4 to 5.1 percent jump in structural unemployment. As further proof of the impact of wage mismatches on employment, the study showed that within the ECCU,

countries like St. Lucia and St. Vincent with persistently high unemployment have much higher unit labor cost than countries
like St. Kitts and Antigua with relatively low unemployment.

If wage mismatches have such a substantial impact on
structural unemployment, it may be fruitful to explore what is
keeping wages artificially elevated in the face of high unemployment.

The Role of Labor Unions and the Public Sector

Strong labor union activity and rigid labor market legislation
have been found to contribute to artificially high wages and thus
high structural unemployment. Apparently, regarding labor
unions, St. Lucia is no exception.

Collective Bargaining Agreements were found to influence
over 80 percent of the labor force of ECCU countries, a share
several fold that of most other regions.[12] The influence and power
of ECCU unions are further augmented by the phenomenon that
most of the major political parties in the region emerged out of
labor unions, and union activism was one of the ways aspiring
politicians established their legitimacy as political leaders and
gained national prominence. For example, the St. Lucia Workers
Union of the 1940s and 1950s gave rise to the St. Lucia Labour
Party, and most of the island's legendary political figures,
including Sir George Charles, Sir John Compton, George Odlum,
and Peter Josie received their baptism of fire into politics through
labor activism. Because of this special relation between unionism
and politics, ECCU labor unions invariably enjoy greater government acceptance and sympathy than they would have otherwise.

The power of unions and their ability to shore up wages are
also bolstered by their membership coverage of key economic
sectors including ports, finance, manufacturing, tourism, and
the public sector. Of those, the public sector is the most critical

because, accounting for a disproportionate share of total employment, its wage negotiations affect most of the labor market. Wage-setting in the public sector has been found to have a significant positive impact on private sector wages, a phenomenon referred to as public sector wage demonstration effects. For instance, increases in public sector wages in response to the aftermath of the Great Recession were followed by substantial increases in private sector wages in St. Lucia.[12]

Labour unions therefore contribute directly to artificially high wages and thus to structural unemployment through collective bargaining, and indirectly through the public sector wage demonstration effect. Similarly, the public sector contributes directly to structural unemployment through its artificially high wages, and indirectly through its impact on reservation wages and its wage demonstration effect.

Solutions

The forgoing discussion may have provided clues on how to tackle the country's high structural unemployment. A partial list may include keeping a lid on public sector wages or linking its wage increases to productivity improvements, reducing or stemming the growth of the public sector, establishing government-labor union nonconfrontational partnerships with the aim to work toward a more rational and harmonious labor market, tailoring education and training to better match job market requirements, fostering a culture of entrepreneurship which may serve as an alternative source of employment for persons with mismatched reservation wages, and raising the productivity of labor.

A country can raise its labor productivity by increasing and improving its stock of physical capital, adopting new or improved technology, and improving the quality of its human resource or, in the jargon of economists, investing in human capital. Human capital can be augmented by education and training, and the cultivation of attitudes and habits conducive to sound business practices.

The good news is that most of these measures have been or are being implemented. In 2013, government established the National Competitiveness and Productivity Council (NCPC) to help foster productivity growth and competitiveness in the country. In recent years the island has been blessed with several new training institutions, both private and public, including Caribbean Hospitality and Tourism Training Institute, National Skills Development Center, Monroe College, and Springboard Training Institute.

A host of apprenticeship/training programs targeting the youth of the country have been established, including Junior Achievement Program, National Apprenticeship Program, Youth Agricultural Entrepreneurship Program, National Summer (Student Training) Program, Hospitality Apprenticeship Program for Youth, and Caribbean Youth Empowerment Program (CYEP).

With telecommunications liberalization, the establishment of the Eastern Caribbean Telecommunications Authority (ECTEL) and the St. Lucia National Telecommunications Regulatory Commission (NTRC), along with a national ICT strategy that includes ICT centers across the island, school computer labs, and universal deployment, ICT technology—the great leveler of the playing field—has become ubiquitous in business, government, schools, and households.[15]

And it appears the government has fostered better relations with the labor unions and is seeking to curb public sector wage increases. For example, responding to the economic downturn in the aftermath of the Great Recession, the Kenny Anthony-led SLP government persuaded the St. Lucia Trade Union Federation to agree to a public sector wage freeze for the April 2013 to March 2016 period, which is in keeping with the IMF structural adjustment advice of stemming the growth of the public sector wage bill by public employment attrition and tying wage increases only to inflation. [16,17] Of course, the IMF prescription was probably only meant to address the size of government recurring expenditures; however, as discussed earlier, curtailing public sector wage increases and the size of the public sector also have the additional effect of curbing reservation wages and keeping private sector labor compensation in check through the demonstration effect.

The bad news is that it does not appear that these programs are part of a well-coordinated effort to reduce unemployment to below a targeted level. The suspicion is that each administration introduces some measures to impress upon voters that it is tackling the country's unemployment ills, but often failing to continue programs started by the previous administration or being arbitrarily dismissive of them.

Even if these programs were to resolve the mismatches and remedy the labor productivity constraints mentioned above, meaning workers' skills were brought in line with market requirements, worker compensation was aligned with labor productivity, and reservation wages became congruous with prevailing market wages, the country may still face significant structural unemployment because it may not be generating sufficient economic activity to employ the entire labor force.

When an economy suffers from enduring low aggregate demand or low level of economic activity and cannot provide full employment, many of the unemployed become disenchanted and exit the labor force. In the process they may never gain requisite job skills or their job skills may become rusty and obsolete. Thus they may be rendered unemployable, thereby bolstering the structural unemployment statistic. In brief, persistently low levels of economic activity create structural unemployment and induce a culture of joblessness, which then becomes accepted as the norm, something not much can be done about.

This suggests that, besides the remedies hinted above, to alleviate the country's structural unemployment problems, there is a need to dimension the economy. And in that regard, small size has its advantages. At the very least, it should make central planning a less complicated task. Technocrats in the departments of statistics, economic planning and industry would have a clear picture of the country's unemployment situation, including the growth, composition, education, and skills of its labor force, i.e., they would know how many people are unemployed, how many school leavers enter the job market each year, and how many workers and the category of workers each sector employs. Therefore, government can estimate how many new jobs and the different categories of jobs that need to be created to bring the economy to full employment, and then determine the size and configuration of enterprises — how many new hotels, factories, informatics enterprises, silicon-like valleys, agricultural and food processing enterprises, etc., — that could accomplish that goal. Armed with this intelligence, government can then formulate strategies and incentive regimes and execute plans of action to make full employment a reality.

There needs to be a fresh approach, a different way of thinking, to solving the country's unemployment ills. So far, it seems the country has approached the problem in a piecemeal, disjointed, and uncoordinated fashion, without well stated performance targets and timeframes. Governments seem satisfied with just being able to do something. However, what is required is a dedicated, comprehensive, concerted plan of action that spans administrations and is invariant to them.

Given the country's starting point, achieving a full employment economy is arguably a daunting task but not an impossible one. Right here in its neighborhood there are countries that have been able to reduce their unemployment rate to levels comparable to that of the developed countries. Take Barbados, for example. During the 1991-1998 period, it experienced an average annual unemployment rate of 19.1 percent, higher than St. Lucia's corresponding average annual unemployment rate of 17.7 percent. However, the fortunes of Barbados turned around. For the next 20 years (1999-2019), it enjoyed an average annual unemployment rate of 10.1 percent, compared to 19.1 percent for St. Lucia.[18]

Now, as has been mentioned several times before, it is customary to blame St. Lucia's economic and social plight on limited resources. But to repeat. *Often the bottleneck is not one of lack of resources, or lack of know-how, or even lack of plans, but one of lack of will and desire.* As mentioned above, a good case in point, which may be worth retelling, regards secondary school education. For decades the country endured significant numbers of its primary school leavers being denied access to a secondary education because the country was supposedly too poor to provide secondary school spaces for all children who so desired. Yet in less than a decade (1997-2006) the Kenny Anthony government established so many additional secondary schools that the talk has shifted from under-capacity to overcapacity, and the problem now facing primary school leavers is not whether they can attend a secondary school but which secondary school they will attend.

As was done for universal secondary education, so can be done for full employment, such that the question that would face school leavers is not whether they will find a job, but what kind of job they will find and in what sector.

Moreover, SLP is likely to give itself a much better chance of ousting the Chastanet government if, besides the Chastanet Ultimatum and the Chastanet-must-go slogan, it includes in its campaign platform a vision and plan to bring the country to full employment. After all, according to the State of Urgency Poll, voters view unemployment as the most critical issue facing the country.

16

THE NECESSITY OF CONSTITUTIONAL REFORM

The State of Urgency Poll suggests that voters view quality of leadership and corruption as two of the most critical issues facing the country, and that taking strong action against corruption and implementing constitutional reform were the two most important changes that the government needed to undertake to improve the way it operates. Therefore, consistent with the often-repeated premise that *our failure to adequately address the nation's most critical problems has more to do with will and desire than lack of resources or know-how*, the quality and integrity of the country's political leadership may lie at the center of the inability to resolve many of its socio-economic problems. Furthermore, considering that the constitution lends itself to extractive institutions and corruption and that according to Acemoglu and Robinson[1] extractive, as opposed to inclusive, institutions invariably lead to economic impoverishment, constitutional reform may be one of the most effective means of curbing corruption, improving the quality and integrity of the political leadership, and setting the country on the path to socio-economic progress. Hence the reason constitutional reform, as opposed to

Chastanet-must-go, may be the most important issue facing the nation.

This chapter revisits the nature of political and economic institutions to determine why and how extractive institutions undermine economic progress and to identify the features of the St. Lucia constitution conducive to extractive political institutions; and how these features enable corruption and extractive economic policies and conduct. Then it examines the cost to the nation of such extractive institutions and discusses how the constitution can be reformed to realize a more inclusive political and economic system with the hope of reducing corruption and fostering more accountable, representative, and conscientious political leaders.

Acemoglu and Robinson[1] posit that differences among nations in economic prosperity can be convincingly explained not by geography, culture, or knowledge of economics or lack thereof, but by the political and economic institutions history bequeathed them. Political and economic institutions are either inclusive or extractive.

Inclusive economic institutions foster broad-based participation in economic activities and allow individuals and entities the freedom to make economic choices. Inclusive economic institutions engender economic progress through inclusive markets that embody freedom of choice, level playing field, and protection of property rights; and through facilitating and embracing technological change, which is considered an engine of sustained economic growth. Extractive economic institutions extract income and wealth from one subset of society (normally the majority) to benefit a different subset (normally a minority political elite).

Inclusive political institutions are centralized and are pluralistic in that power is broadly distributed and is subject to checks and constraints. Extractive political institutions obtain when power is absolutist, i.e., the distribution of power is narrow and unconstrained, and/or when there is a lack of political centralization or state centralization.

According to the theory, nations or regions with inclusive political and economic institutions tend to prosper, while those with extractive political and economic institutions eventually become impoverished.

As mentioned in Chapter 2, the West Indies slave plantation system was a typical example of an extractive political and economic system. The white minority enjoyed absolutist political power with few constraints and the slave plantation economy was designed to extract all surplus production beyond subsistence at the expense of the slaves for the benefit of the white minority.

Slavery was abolished in 1838, but the extractive political and economic institutions remained. Therefore, in the colonial era, the society continued extracting from the black majority for the benefit of the white minority, thus the vast majority of the population languished in poverty.

St. Lucia became independent in 1979, so it is tempting to conclude (with slavery gone and the country now squarely in the hands of duly elected representatives of the masses and as such can be described as a democratic state) that it now enjoys inclusive political and economic institutions. However, a democratic state, meaning a state ruled by elected representatives, does not necessarily imply inclusive political and economic institutions. Colombia and Argentina are two democratic states with regular general elections but which, according to Acemoglu and Robinson,[1] have major elements of extractive institutions that limit their economic progress.

St. Lucia enjoys an inclusive political process in that the populace participates in the election of the governing political party or administration. But once that administration is in power, it faces few restraints and checks and balances on its power. So it basically has a free rein. The prime minister faces even fewer restraints, and seemingly enjoys unfettered power, so much so that many view the Office of the Prime Minister as a dictatorship, and parliamentary governments have been referred to as elective dictatorships.[2] Therefore, once a party is in power, it becomes an absolutist government and hence an extractive political institution. The government also becomes an extractive economic agent because it extracts income and wealth from the general population for the benefit of its clique that may include Cabinet ministers, other political appointees, their family and friends, and selected party supporters. Later, the chapter will delve into the different ways St. Lucian governments have gone about extracting income and resources from the populace and the cost to the country of such practices.

Extractive Institutions and Economic Regression

Right up to the 18th century, most of Europe was ruled by absolutist governments comprising the monarchs and the nobility or aristocracy. These extractive political systems established extractive economic institutions in which the ruling elite owned most of the land which served as a major source of income, and they enjoyed trading monopolies granted by the crown and maintained by the imposition of entry barriers. The ruling elites resisted economic progress — the introduction of new technologies, the establishment of factories, and, in general, industrialization — because it meant workers would leave the land to secure employment in the towns, causing land rents to fall, and farm wages to rise. It also meant that the novel enterprises and modes of production attracted new entrepreneurs and merchants who eroded the trading privileges of the elite. Besides the economic losses the elites suffered, they were also faced with the prospect of diminishing political power. The buildup of the population into towns facilitated organized action and communication among workers thus the populace was less easily controlled, and the new class of business owners with their rising wealth was better positioned to make inroads into the political power of the traditional elites.

This brings to mind the concept of creative destruction first coined by economist Joseph Schumpter[3] and embraced by Acemoglu and Robinson. According to this theory, economic growth and technological change are invariably accompanied by losers and winners as new technology displaces the old, new sectors draw resources away from established ones, new firms take business away from incumbents, and new technologies render existing skills and machines obsolete, and as the new entrants gain political clout at the expense of the political power of established elites.

Acemoglu and Robinson[4] present many examples across history and geography of the ramifications of extractive institutions. A look at a few of these examples within the context of the adoption of technology and creative destruction may help illustrate how such institutions can impede economic progress.

Knitting Machine

The first example pertains to sixteenth-century England during the reign of Elizabeth I (1558-1603) when she decreed that her subjects must always wear a knitted cap. As was to be expected, the decree brought knitted caps in high demand. Watching his mother and sisters knitting caps in the evenings, William Lee, a graduate of Cambridge University and a local priest in Calverton, England, had an epiphany. "If garments were made by two needles and one line of thread, why not several needles to take up the thread?" Gripped with the idea of a machine that would free people from the drudgery of hand knitting, Lee neglected his "duties to church and family" and completed his invention of the "stock frame" knitting machine in 1589. He then traveled to London hoping to meet with Queen Elizabeth to demonstrate the usefulness of his invention and to apply for a patent.

Queen Elizabeth was not amused. She said, "Thou aimest high, Master Lee. Consider thou what the invention could do to my poor subjects. It would assuredly bring to them ruin by depriving them of employment, thus making them beggars."

Deflated but undeterred — after all, the invention had consumed him day and night— Lee moved to France, hoping for better luck. But the results were the same. When he returned to England, he presented his case to James I, Elizabeth's successor, but the King refused him for the same reason as had the Queen.

Ostensibly, the monarchs used concern for their subjects as the reason for their decision. However, what drove them to reject the invention had more to do with safeguarding their rule than with their subjects' best interest. They viewed the "stock frame" knitting machine as a threat to their royal power. They reasoned that the invention would put people out of work and create discontentment and political instability. Meaning, the creative destruction wrought by the invention would make knitters economic losers and the monarchs political losers. Protecting their power therefore took precedence over the induced productivity gains of the invention, which in the long run, as other such inventions proved, could have benefited society greatly.

Printing Press

Johannes Gutenberg of Mainz, Germany, invented the movable-type printing press in 1445. Before then books were hand-copied by scribes or block-printed with each page printed with its own specifically prepared block of wood. Accordingly, books were rare and expensive. Gutenberg's invention changed all that. Books became readily available and more affordable and as such induced mass literacy and education. Within a few decades, the printing press spread throughout Europe.

But the Ottoman Empire presented a different story. Beginning in 1485 with sultan Bayezid II, a succession of Ottoman sultans banned Muslims from printing in Arabic. Consequently, literacy in Ottoman territories lagged far behind that of most European countries. For example, in 1800 only 2 to 3 percent of Ottoman citizens were believed to be literate, whereas in England 60 percent of men and 40 percent of women were literate.

Books and literacy help spread knowledge and herald economic development and progress, so why did the ruling elites of the Ottoman Empire choose to miss out on such a good thing? According to Acemoglu and Robinson, as a highly absolutist empire with accompanying extractive institutions, books were a threat to the power of the Ottoman ruling elite. Books disseminate ideas and help raise consciousness and thus make people less controllable. Some of the ideas may be subversive and challenge the prevailing social and political order. Moreover, since books make knowledge more readily available, they help undermine the authority of ruling elites, one of whose source of power was the control of knowledge.

Factories and Railways

The Glorious Revolution in 1688 dismantled absolutist rule in Britain and bought about inclusive political and economic institutions, which facilitated the Industrial Revolution (1760-1840) and its accompanying unprecedented economic growth. At the time of the Industrial Revolution, Habsburg and Russia were still under absolutist rule with extractive economic institutions based on feudalism and serfdom. In sharp contrast to Britain, which did not only embrace the technological breakthroughs of the time but led the Industrial Revolution, the ruling elites of Habsburg and Russia opposed social and technological advancement, including the establishment of factories and railways.

Why? Industry and factories draw workers from the countryside to the cities, thereby upsetting the feudal order, the cornerstone of Habsburg's and Russia's extractive economic institutions. The concentration of people in cities provides a ready audience for those seeking to subvert absolutism. Railways foster the free movement of people and hence ideas and make people harder to control or restrain.

A couple of anecdotes may further clarify the motivation behind the ruling elite's opposition to progress. When the Austrian government was urged to introduce social reform for improving the lot of the poor, a government official responded with: "We do not desire at all that the great masses shall become well off and independent... How could we otherwise rule over them?"

Besides banning the establishment of new factories in Vienna, when a proposal to build a northern railway was presented to Francis I, the Austria-Hungary emperor (1804-1835), he said: "No, no, I will have nothing to do with it, lest the revolution might come into the country."

International Trade

The world has China to thank for several major inventions including clocks, the compass, gunpowder, paper and paper money, silk and porcelain, and blast furnaces for making cast iron. In addition, China independently invented the spinning wheel and water power. At the time Christopher Columbus set sail on his first voyage to the New World, China's shipbuilding and seafaring were probably just as advanced as that of Europe. In the early 1400s, Emperor Yongle sponsored six large trade missions to Southeast and South Asia, Arabia, and Africa. One of the fleets comprised 27,800 men, 62 large treasure ships, and 190 smaller ships. The expedition's large ships were multiple times larger than the Santa Maria, Columbus's flagship. Yet after 1436, subsequent emperors banned all overseas trade and the building of seagoing ships. A ban that would remain in effect until 1567.

Despite the dire economic consequences of the ban, the emperors took this decision because they feared that as international trade enriched merchants, they would become emboldened and challenge the country's absolutist rule. Thus, the emperors sacrificed economic progress for upholding their absolutist rule and for political and social stability.

However, their ban on international trade had consequences beyond economics. Instead of China, it was Europe with its adventurous seafaring that conquered the world, and it was English, not Mandarin, that became the universal language. It was Europe, and not the other way around, that, beginning with the first Opium War in the 19th century, subjugated China, a phenomenon attributed largely to China's weakness at sea and failure in naval warfare.

One may be tempted to conclude that the examples given above are farfetched when viewed from the St. Lucian context. After all, St. Lucia is a democracy and is not ruled by monarchs, sultans, emperors and other such dictators. But closer examination may reveal that the examples are not far removed from the St. Lucian reality.

Is it by coincidence that government and businesses are keener to sponsor events like carnival and other forms of *bakanal* that appeal to the senses than activities like literature, theater, etc., that raise consciousness? Or is it because thinking and conscious people are harder to control and manipulate and are more likely to oppose irregularities?

How many foreign enterprises that would have brought jobs and economic wellbeing to the country, but which never materialized because politicians demanded bribes? How many projects started by outgoing governments that incoming governments aborted because all the monies to pass hands had already been passed, so there was little financial gain to the new players of continuing the projects, and/or because they would not have gained political mileage from the projects since they were already credited to the outgoing administration?

Why, despite the obvious inefficiencies, has government structured its conduct of business like a mafia organization, such that the most insignificant of transactions requires ministerial or permanent secretarial signatures, or to get any movement on just about anything one has to make a ministerial visit—requesting of the godfather favors and paying homage for services rendered? Is it to cement their hold on the electorate, highlight their indispensability, display their power?

Was it because St. Lucians were too poor to afford universal secondary education that generation upon generation of citizens missed out on secondary education? Or was it because the existing government viewed universal secondary education as a threat to its hold on power? If not, how does one explain that as soon as a new government came into power, with one stroke of the pen secondary education was open to all? If this suspicion seems farfetched, consider that a Cabinet minister of that era, reportedly said: "If we give them secondary and university education, they will not appreciate us and they will soon remove us from power."[5] And if one is still unconvinced, consider that one of the alleged and much talked about salient features of Compton's rule was the deliberate neglect or punishment of communities that had a history of not voting UWP. The story is told of the 1987 elections when the UWP government deposited electric poles in Laborie, a Labour stronghold, ostensibly to provide residents with electricity and thus sway them to vote UWP, only to carry away the poles when the election results pronounced UWP the overall victor but proclaimed SLP the winner in Laborie.

Salient Features of St. Lucia's System of Government[6]

St. Lucia has a parliamentary system of government in which the monarch of the United Kingdom, represented by the governor general, is the head of state. The government comprises a Parliament and a Cabinet. The Parliament comprises the governor general (as the monarch's representative), the Senate and the House of Assembly.

The Senate comprises 11 senators, appointed by the governor general: 6 on the advice of the prime minister, 3 on the advice of the opposition leader, and 2 at the discretion of the governor general after consulting with religious, economic or social organizations that may serve as sources of Senate selection.

The House of Assembly comprises the elected constituency representatives (17 in total), a Speaker (who may or may not be an elected district representative), and the attorney general, since the office of attorney general was declared (by Statutory Instrument 41/1997) a public office as opposed to the office of a minister. Parliament serves as the legislative branch of government and as such the constitution grants it the power to make laws, and to make alterations to the constitution and the Supreme Court Order.

The power in Parliament lies principally with the House of Assembly. The Senate can introduce bills (excluding appropriation bills) or present amendment to bills, but the passage of bills and amendment to bills, or alterations to the constitution and the Supreme Court Order, require the House of Assembly final vote.

The Cabinet is the executive branch of government and it comprises the prime minister, other ministers, and the attorney general (since it is a public office). The prime minister is appointed by the governor general as a member of the House whom the governor general believes can command the support of the majority of House members. The other ministers are appointed (from the Senate and the House) by the governor general on the advice of the prime minister. The constitution stipulates that the function of Cabinet is to advise the governor general in the government of the country, and that the Cabinet is responsible to Parliament for such advice, suggesting that Cabinet is accountable or answerable to Parliament and Parliament is charged with providing Cabinet with oversight.

The governor general must "remove the prime minister from office if a resolution of no confidence in the government is passed by the House and the prime minister does not within 3 days either resign from his or her office or advise the governor general to dissolve Parliament." The governor general may also remove the prime minister from office if, following a general election, changes in House membership suggest the prime minister cannot command the support of a majority of House members.

The judiciary represents St. Lucia's third branch of government and besides protecting the fundamental rights and freedoms of citizens it serves as a check and restraint on the powers of the executive and the legislature, the other two branches of government. St. Lucia's judiciary comprises the magistracy (district courts), the Eastern Caribbean Supreme Court, and the Privy Council. The Eastern Caribbean Supreme Court comprises a Court of Appeal and a High Court of Justice. The Supreme Court is headquartered in St. Lucia, but each member state has its own court office.[7]

Most criminal cases are heard and decided in the magistrate courts, however, the more serious cases, including those pertaining to fundamental rights and freedoms, and constitutional matters, are dispensed with in the High Courts, which have unlimited jurisdiction over civil and criminal matters. The Court of Appeal performs the appellate function of the Supreme Court. It is itinerant—travels to member states and territories to hear appeals from the judgments of the magistrate courts, high courts, and special courts on both civil and criminal matters. The Privy Council of the UK, which, excluding the UK itself, was once the court of last resort for the entire British Empire, serves as St. Lucia's final appellate court.

Headquartered in Trinidad, the Caribbean Court of Justice (CCJ),[8] ratified by CARICOM member states, came into effect

April 16, 2005. The CCJ represents an alternative to the Privy Council as the court of last appeal for member states. So far Barbados, Belize, and Guyana have replaced the Privy Council with the CCJ as their final appellate court.

The Judicial and Legal Services Commission (JLSC) is responsible for the discipline and dismissal of magistrates, while the Minister of Justice is responsible for the day-to-day management of their operations. In contrast to the Supreme Court, the effectiveness and integrity of the magistracy have been brought to question and there appears to be a lack of public trust in its dispensation. Yet the public's perception of the justice system may be largely formed by its contact with the lower courts since they represent its most common interface with the judiciary. The shortcomings of the lower court have been attributed to several factors, including (1) the joint management of the magistracy by the JLSC and the Minister for Justice has created management ambiguity and unclear lines of responsibility; (2) the magistrates do not enjoy the security of tenure and the level of independence afforded the Supreme Court judges; and (3) the financial resources at the disposal of the magistracy may be inadequate for its proper functioning.[9]

In discussing St. Lucia's system of government, one would be remiss to exclude local government, which is considered an effective means of delivering public goods and services to the populace and ensuring government policies reach all communities.[9] St. Lucia has enjoyed intermittent periods of local government, the last of which was suspended in 1979. Since then the councilors serving on town and village councils are nominated by the government along party lines, thus the councils are not politically independent bodies but are extensions of the party in power. In 1997, the Labour government established a task force on re-instituting and strengthening local government. One recommendation of the task force was that initially local governments should focus on such basic services as maintaining and repairing cemeteries, roads, squares, parks, beaches and open spaces, sporting facilities, and public buildings; issuing licenses and permits; and operating such facilities as libraries. Upon maturity local governments can then extend their scope of operation to include land use planning, operating and maintaining libraries and schools, providing primary health care, assisting the disadvantaged with housing, and serving as an advisor to central government. The task force presented its findings and recommendations in a green paper and conducted public consultations on local government reform, but the reform process went no further.

However, besides serving as an effective means of delivering public goods and services to the populace and ensuring government policies reach all communities, elected local governments can contribute to the balance and devolution of power from the center to the periphery. Therefore, elected local government is a step toward greater democracy and a more inclusive political system.

Extractive Political and Economic Institutions

The government displays elements of an extractive political institution. Power is concentrated in Cabinet, the executive branch, which faces few checks and restraints on its power. Parliament is supposed to provide Cabinet with oversight, but Cabinet ministers are mostly appointed from among the ruling party's House members, and when this source is exhausted the other ministers are appointed from among the ruling party's appointed senators. This suggests a lack of independence or separation of power between the executive and the legislature since the district representatives of the ruling party form both the Cabinet and the House . It also suggests a lack of accountability, since a majority of members of Parliament, who are supposed to provide Cabinet with oversight, are themselves in Cabinet, meaning both executive and legislative powers are embodied in the same persons, therefore Cabinet is answerable only to itself. This characteristic of the Cabinet voids one of the most effective means of preventing the abuse of power — countervailing powers simultaneously keeping each other in check. The power of Parliament should have been able to check that of Cabinet. But as constituted, this is not the case.

To further clarify, take, for example, the prime minister comes to Parliament seeking approval to enter a contractual arrangement with a developer. However, the majority of House members are not only of the ruling party but are themselves Cabinet ministers. Therefore, the prime minister seeking the approval of Parliament, a requirement to serve as a check and restraint on Cabinet, is tantamount to Cabinet seeking the approval of Cabinet, thus the prime minister and his Cabinet operate with virtually no checks and constraints on their power.

This brings to mind what former St. Lucia ambassador, Earl Huntley,[10,11] has pointed out as the incompatibility of the UK parliamentary system with the St. Lucia reality, hence the need for constitutional reform. Consider, for example, that the current Allen Chastanet Cabinet comprises 14 ministers, 11 of whom are drawn from a House of Assembly of only 17 elected members. Since the Cabinet is drawn largely from the House, it will always mean that there will be few House members left on the bench to provide Cabinet independent oversight, and also that the executive and the legislature will be largely populated by the same persons. With the UK, the picture changes. Like St. Lucia, the Cabinet is formed largely from the House of Commons (the UK equivalent of the House of Assembly), but compared to St. Lucia's 17 elected member-strong House of Assembly, the House of Commons comprises 650 elected members from which a Cabinet of around 20 members (24 at the present) is drawn, leaving plenty of bench members available for forming special committees and for providing Cabinet with oversight.[12] The relatively small size of St.

Lucia's government therefore makes it incompatible with this feature of the UK's parliamentary system.

Extractive political institutions invariably give rise to extractive economic institutions and behavior. So it may be instructive to look at how Cabinet as an extractive political institution has led to extractive economic practices and the resultant price St. Lucia has had to pay.

To begin, consider the following observation of the Constitutional Reform Commission.[9]

> Given the fusion of power and the small size of the Parliament itself, the legislative branch of government has not been able to effectively check Cabinet to ensure that the executive branch does not engage in hasty policy making that is designed to achieve short-term popularity of their policy proposals...given the extensive concentration of power and swiftness with which decisions can be reached, it is fraught with danger... There is no security for due reflection, no opportunity for second thoughts. Errors may be irretrievable...it (is) near impossible (for Parliament) to engage in any form of meaningful scrutiny of government business."

In a nutshell, the Commission revealed that Cabinet is left to its own devices to conduct business as it sees fit, with little scrutiny, accountability, and checks and restraints. One consequence of this reality is that prime ministers have formed a habit of committing the country to multi-million-dollar transactions, sometimes with disastrous consequences, without the consent of their Cabinet and sometimes without even their full awareness.

The Rochamel affair[13,14] is one case in point. Shortly after taking office in 1997, prime minister Kenny Anthony committed the government as guarantor for a Royal Merchant Bank loan of US$12.75 million to help purchase the Hyatt Regency Rochamel Development (now Sandals Grande) at Pigeon Island Causeway. The investor defaulted on the loan, so the government had to pay the bank US$14.59 million for principal and accumulated interest.

According to the commission of inquiry[14] into the matter, the loan guarantee agreement had no provisions for the government to be rewarded with shares in the development, nor was there any attempt to safeguard the country from potential loss, so the loan repayment was a net loss to St. Lucia. The inquiry also revealed that government provided no oversight of the project, there was no evidence that any Cabinet minister or any other high-level government official was involved in the decision-making process. The prime minister was the only signatory on all documents pertaining to the loan guarantee. In fact, details of the transaction only came to light when the prime minister faced Parliament to secure finance for the loan repayment and at the proceedings of the commission of inquiry.

The circumstances of the Rochamel affair beg the question: Why would Prime Minister Dr. Kenny Anthony enter (what the evidence suggests is) a clandestine transaction that puts the country at risk for no apparent gain? If, as ostensibly presented, the transaction was all for preserving and protecting St. Lucian jobs, why the secrecy, why did the prime minister feel compelled to get no one else involved? Maybe if the prime minister had involved Cabinet ministers, legal advisers, economic and financial planners, and other senior-level government officials in the decision-making process, the agreement would have included, at the very least, a clause assigning shares to the government commensurate with the loan repayment in the event of default.

The Grynberg affair,[15,16] in which the then prime minister, Kenny Anthony, signed a hydrocarbon exploration agreement in 2000 with Jack Grynberg and his RSM Production Corporation, represents an even more blatant abuse of prime ministerial power than Rochamel. Because not only did the prime minister enter the contractual arrangement in secret, not bothering to seek the consultation and consent of even his Cabinet, but he violated the Minerals (Vesting) Act which stipulates that no one may mine any minerals without a license granted by the governor general; and a person shall not prospect for or mine any minerals unless allowed by the governor general with a grant of license. The governor general has since (reportedly) noted that she had no personal or firsthand knowledge of the agreement between the prime minister and Grynberg, nor had anyone engaged her on the subject in her official capacity. Yet at the time the prime minister was signing the mineral exploration contract, Grenada was in litigation with RSM over a similar agreement. St. Lucia eventually terminated the agreement with RSM, compelling Jack Grynberg to file a breach of contract claim with the International Centre for Settlement of Investment Disputes (ICSID) seeking reliance damage. So far, the case has cost the government about US$2 million in legal fees.

Chapters 7 to 11, examined how Allen Chastanet and his Cabinet may have abused their unfettered power, seemingly running roughshod over the country, denigrating its laws and statutory bodies, undermining its sovereignty, and being dismissive of its natural and cultural patrimony. In this regard it may be illuminating to revisit the DSH arrangement—in which the government agreed to hand over the nation's sovereignty (a foreign entity was charged with selling its passports) and some of its most vital and strategic assets to a foreign entity with no clear indication of what the country would gain in return—to highlight not only the abuse of power but the cavalier use of power.

A mere three months in office, the prime minister, Allen Chastanet, signed a development proposal agreement[17] with Teo Ah Khing and Desert Star Holdings that the former Kenny Anthony-led administration had spent 18 months wrestling with but was yet to arrive at a satisfactory arrangement. Dr. Kenny Anthony has since revealed that the agreement Allen Chastanet signed represented the starting point of his administration's negotiations with the developer and by the time of the 2016 elections his administration had made significant strides toward a negotiated agreement more advantageous to the country. As if the swiftness with which Allen Chastanet signed what many considered an atrocious agreement was not cavalier enough, it was reported that some of his Cabinet ministers admitted they had endorsed the agreement without ever reading it, making one wonder whether the prime minister himself had read and understood the agreement before offering his signature. What can be a more cavalier exercise of power than to sign away the country's sovereignty and patrimony without bothering to read and decipher the agreement?

The cavalier abuse of power did not stop there. For a development of such magnitude (billed at US$3.0 billion) that would transform Vieux Fort beyond recognition, that would mean the abandonment of a national stadium and a newly-built and yet to be used multi-million dollar abattoir, the expensive decommisioning and relocation of a landfill, the loss of a government training and experimental farm and hundreds of acres of cattle grazing land, and that would involve the relocation of several hundred Vieux Fort residents, one would think before rushing ahead the government would conduct public consultations, gain awareness of the community's concerns and reservations, etc. Instead of such consultations, the prime minister's attitude was akin to: *Vieux Fortians must stop complaining and protesting. They should be thankful and ecstatic about the project, for it will be like the "time of the Americans" all over again. After all Kenny Anthony didn't do anything for the district, so it's just bush, ghettos, and joblessness in Vieux Fort.*

In fact, nothing seemed able to dissuade the prime minister from this course of action. Not the environmental concerns of the St. Lucia National Trust, not the reservations of the CIP and of Invest St. Lucia (the agency charged with sourcing foreign investment) about the financial viability of the development, not the protest marches of Vieux Fort residents, and not the clearly and loudly articulated apprehensions of the Vieux Fort Concerned Citizens Coalition for Change (VFCCCC). The only concession the government made was to belatedly and pretentiously hold townhall meetings to counteract Vieux Fort's protest marches, symposiums, and public meetings.

Today, after millions of taxpayers' dollars have been poured into the project,[18] after the construction of a horse racetrack and the building of a new road (estmated road cost: $EC13.6 million) to accommodate the racetrack, after the decommission of the landfill (estimated cost: $EC15.5 million) in the way of the development, it appears the developer, Teo Ah Khing, has lost interest and the development is floundering, leaving the public clueless about what is happening, and forcing them to wonder whether the DSH development is heading the same way of the Le Paradis environmental disaster.

Governments' abuse of power continues to cost the nation dearly.

Media reports of alleged government corruption and wrongdoing and the investigation conducted in Part III, Chapters 7-12, on why the Chastanet-led UWP government is viewed by some to be the worst government in St. Lucia's history, provide insights into the ways prime ministers and their Cabinets have used their unrestrained power to engage in economic extraction at tremendous cost to the nation.

Earlier it was mentioned that government ministers may have formed a habit of requiring bribes, in the manner of booking agents charging commissions, from foreign enterprises seeking to do business in St. Lucia. On the surface, this kind of corruption seems to impact just the foreign enterprises by raising their cost of doing business. However, it is a form of economic extraction in that while it fills the pockets of the politicians, it leaves the country worse off. The higher cost of doing business makes the country less competitive in attracting foreign capital and discourages businesses from making a home on the island. It affects the mix of foreign enterprises in the country because it is only those able and willing to pay the ministerial bribes that will end up investing; but these enterprises may have less to offer and may not be best for the development of the country. Furthermore, corruption at this the highest level of government has externality effects. It can help permeate a pattern of corruption throughout the government system, from ministry department officers to customs officers to police officers. Therefore, as an extractive economic practice, the ministers' bribe or rent-seeking behavior can directly and indirectly retard the country's economic progress. The unsettling feeling is that one can never be sure of the ultimate cost to the country of this practice.

To discern the patterns of government economic extraction, it is important to note that because of disbursement protocols, including required signatures, Cabinet ministers cannot pocket government funds through direct access to such sources as the Treasury and the Consolidated Fund. So by default government projects have become one of the key instruments of economic extraction. To begin with, increasingly the bidding process is being bypassed and the projects are direct awards, which allow governments to award projects not necessarily to the most efficacious contractors or bids but to those who present them with the greatest opportunity for personal gain. Moreover, since the projects are direct awards, there is no competition on the basis of cost, quality, and delivery timeframe. Therefore, the country is likely to incur higher costs (than otherwise) for inferior deliverables. The reported overpriced direct awards of the Babonneau Highway and Desruisseaux Road rehabilitation projects to Asphalt and Mining Company (A&M) upon the alleged request of Minister Guy Joseph, seems an excellent illustration of the above strategy. Apparently, public works run-away cost is so pervasive that St.

Lucia's everyday vocabulary has broadened to include "cost overrun."

When government cannot get away with direct purchase and is forced to employ the bidding process, there are creative ways to still end up with the contractor of choice, as Minister Guy Joseph may have demonstrated in the Hewanorra International Airport Redevelopment Project.

With Fresh Start (see Chapter 11), it seems the government may have gone further in its use of projects for economic extraction, because not only has it been assigning projects to Fresh Start by direct awards, it has, according to some experts, illegally provided the company fiscal incentives, including exemption from corporate income tax.

But how do government ministers profit from such ventures? Well, once the contracts are awarded to the "right" operatives, it is a matter of finding creative ways to channel kickbacks, which can take the form of jobs for cronies and political supporters, payment-in-kind, campaign finance contributions, cash kickbacks, etc. And what is the economic cost to the nation of such corruption?

First, as with Fresh Start, there is a direct loss of income from revenues forgone because of the income tax, import duty, and excise tax exemptions. Second, since projects do not go through a bidding process and their costs are likely padded with set-asides for kickbacks, taxpayers are paying more than they need to for public works and such works may be of inferior quality than if conducted in the absence of corruption. Besides these economic costs, there are social costs associated with this kind of corruption that further drags the country down economically. Former independent senator, Everistus Jn Marie, said it best when referring to the Fresh Start situation. He noted that such practices create a culture of "illegality, corruption, and crime"[19] and will lead to impoverishment.

The Tuxedo scandal[16] represents another variant of the use of government concessions for economic extraction. In July 2007, under the Tourism Incentives Act, the Stephenson King-led Cabinet gave Health Minister, Keith Mondesir, duty-free concessions on imports of materials for the refurbishment of his 10 villas and restaurants referred to as Tuxedo Villas. However, the minister violated the terms and conditions of the concessions when he used the Cabinet approval as cover to import items for his household, which had no discernable connection with and was not adjacent to his tourism plant. The scandal took another twist when, obviously to protect the minister from a customs department probe into the matter, in June 2008 the Cabinet of ministers retroactively extended the concessions to include Mondesir's residence.

The Supreme Court was not fooled nor amused by Cabinet's attempt at coverup, nor did it harbor any doubt that Mondesir and the Cabinet had used the concessions as an instrument of economic extraction. In its deliberations, the Court noted that Cabinet "cannot make decisions that result in reducing the revenue that the government is entitled to collect in any arbitrary and cavalier manner, especially where the decisions benefit one of its own members..." And that the decision to offer the concession retroactively "represented a blatant conflict of interest ... outrageous in its defiance of logic and accepted moral standards."

Public works contracts as an instrument of economic extraction can take an even more sinister turn. As hinted earlier, the suspicion is that newly elected governments are often reluctant to continue projects started under the former administration because apparently most of the opportunities for economic extraction occur at the start of projects when contracts are awarded and so there is little to be gained by the new government. Sometimes, rather than continuing a project already in progress, administrations prefer to abort it and then initiate a new project to serve the same purpose but under the guise of a different name and different objectives. The abortion of the Vieux Fort Administrative Complex (where a new WASCO building is now under construction), the reformulation of the St. Lucia Jazz Festival, the abandonment of SLP's Hewanorra International Airport PPP concept to be replaced by an alternative approach more conducive to economic extraction, and the demolishing of part of the newly built St. Jude Hospital to be replaced with a new structure that dwarfs the preexisting complex may all be part of that phenomenon.

Indeed, for a prime minister who ran on a campaign platform of a savvy businessman ready to roll up his sleeves and get to work, it is amazing that Allen Chastanet has been more about aborting projects and dismantling programs than about initiating them. So much so, that while most citizens can upon demand quickly scroll up a list of projects, programs, and government-funded institutions the prime minister has either scaled down or abandoned (see Part III), they are hard-pressed to come up with even one or two projects or programs he has initiated.

The St. Jude reconstruction project, which so far has spanned three administrations and still counting, presents an interesting case study of (suspicious) economic extraction. As revealed by Untold Stories and a project audit report commissioned in 2016, the hospital was built under an atmosphere of unaccountability and mismanagement. The audit report was characterized as "a catalog of a series of catastrophic engineering, financial, and project management failures."[20]

The prime ministers (who as ministers for finance were ultimately heading the project) and their project management teams were accused of providing little or no project supervision or oversight. There was no approved budget, no approved building plans, no defined scope of work, no DCA approval, no impact assessment study. The project consultant, project manager, and main contractors had no experience in hospital construction. The project was a bonanza for most involved. The project consultant company's fee, which started at EC$277 thousand, ended up totaling EC$11.54 million. The monthly compensation of the lead project consultant increased from EC$38,000 to EC$49,500. The salary of the site engineer, who apparently lacked both the certification, academic qualifications, and "requisite construction supervisory experience," ballooned from EC$9,000 to EC$16,500 per month, with no corresponding increase in responsibilities. Most of the contracts were by direct awards. Work invoices were honored based on "unsubstantiated time inputs."

The project appeared to be a gluttony of waste. Carelessly stored, millions of dollars of purchased and donated specialized medical equipment were rendered useless; hundreds of thousands of dollars were paid for equipment storage when a government storage facility to serve that purpose remained empty; EC$60 thousand was used to pump water out of a building's foundation.

The buildings were not built to hospital specifications. Some doors were too narrow and some rooms were too small to receive or accommodate requisite equipment; operating theaters were too small to serve their purpose; and as if unmindful of the fire that destroyed the hospital and hence the reconstruction, the new structures were considered fire hazards.

In sharp contrast (and very telling), the morgue and ambulance bay, both courtesy of the Mexican government and built outside the management structure of the St. Jude reconstruction project, were the only structures built to hospital specifications and standards and within pre-specified budgets and timeframes.

By the time of the June 2016 general elections, the project that was expected to cost under EC$50 million and completed in less than two years, was over six years in the making with a cost tag that had mushroomed to EC$118 million. Yet, most of the buildings were only about 50 percent completed, external works were about 90% unfinished, several buildings were waiting to get off ground, and originally expected to house 115 beds, it was doubtful that as constructed the hospital would accommodate 70 beds.

Now, 2021, about 12 years since the start of the St. Jude reconstruction project and nearing the end of the term of the third administration to work on the project, the hospital is still far from completion. And as if to put an exclamation mark on the fiasco, the media was informed that on top of the EC$118 million already spent, it will take another EC$100 million to complete the hospital.[21]

Granted, since politicians never self-report misdeeds, one may never be sure whether the St. Jude travesty was a result of economic extraction or gross mismanagement combined with unscrupulous professionals abusing the system or both. But one would have been hard-pressed to devise and implement a project in a manner more ideal for economic extraction.

In his article,[22] *The Economics of Corruption*, Dr. Prosper Raynold, St. Lucian economics professor at Miami University of Ohio, cast further light on the cost of economic extraction. According to Professor Raynold, faced with tight budgets, corrupt governments are likely to give priority to large infrastructure projects over projects associated with education, healthcare, and the maintenance of infrastructure, because large infrastructure projects present greater opportunities for economic extraction and provide more political visibility. This causes misallocation of resources because it leads to overinvestment in large infrastructure projects at the expense of investment in education, healthcare, and the maintenance of infrastructure. Hence economic extraction is often associated with white elephants, poorly constructed roads, bridges, and buildings, poorly maintained roads and government buildings, low quality public healthcare, and poor schooling. Moreover, since education and healthcare are contributing factors to sustained economic growth, underinvestment in these sectors retards economic progress.

Above it was noted that the rent or bribe-seeking behavior of government ministers can discourage foreign investment, but Dr. Raynold informs us that corruption negatively impacts both foreign and domestic investment in physical capital, an unfortunate scenario because this impedes the accumulation of capital which is an important determinant of the rate of economic growth.

Dr. Raynold also indicated that since large firms are better positioned to pay bribes and help finance political campaigns, they are more likely than small and medium size firms to secure political favor, which gives them a competitive advantage to the possible detriment of less advantageously positioned firms. This has serious implications for the economic growth and employment prospects of a country, because small and medium size companies have been found to be the primary drivers of economic growth and new employment; compared to large, established firms, they tend to be more innovative and more active in the introduction of new products and services.

However, what may be most revealing about Professor Raynold's article was the insidiousness of corruption and its tendency to distort economic incentives. Some examples of this kind of distortion include government ranking investments based on political visibility and suitability to economic extraction than on the basis of their contribution to public welfare; citizens contesting constituency elections, not because of burning desires to uplift their communities and country, but for the opportunity to engage in economic extraction as Cabinet ministers; firms focusing more on cultivating political connections and less on production and cost efficiency because of the reality that political connectedness and willingness to pay bribes and provide kickbacks play a bigger role in securing government contracts and favors than the quality and cost-effectiveness of deliverables; and workers choosing to invest less in human capital and more in engendering and maintaining connections because they face work situations in which nepotism, family connections and willingness to grant sexual favors carry more weight in hiring and promotion decisions than do education, training, and experience.

Constitutional Reform

As mentioned at the start, SLP has been saturating the air with Chastanet-must-go and threatening voters with the Chastanet Ultimatum, as if Chastanet is the biggest problem facing St. Lucia. But as has been observed, Chastanet and his UWP administration do not have a monopoly on abuse of power and economic extraction. So voting Chastanet out of office would not solve the problem of governments operating within an extractive constitutional and political structure that lends itself to corruption and economic extraction. Therefore, getting rid of Chastanet is no guarantee that subsequent governments will behave any differently. As discussed in Chapter 2, when the structure-conduct-performance paradigm was invoked, the only lasting solution is to introduce more inclusive institutions through constitutional reform and laws and regulations that preclude the apparent excesses of the Chastanet administration. This conclusion appears to be in line with the thinking of the State of Urgency poll respondents in that they view corruption, quality of leadership, and constitutional reform as some of the most critical issues the country needs to grapple with.

Claudius Francis, a popular St. Lucia talk show host, and an SLP operative who served as president of the Senate in the former Kenny Anthony Administration, begged to differ. In his opinion, there is nothing wrong with the constitution and the structure of government; rather, he believes the problem lies with the integrity of the persons running the country. The talk show host's view seems equivalent to saying that the performance of a car has nothing to do with its engine, aerodynamics, and fuel, but all to do with the driving skills of the person behind the wheel. Obviously, as any NASCAR driver knows, it is both.

As mentioned in previous chapters, there is no shortage of plans, proposals, or ideas on how to remedy the country's problems. Regarding extractive institutions, the government of St. Lucia established the Constitutional Reform Commission in 2005 to "review and reform" the constitution to make government a more democratic, accountable, participatory and inclusive institution. The 348-page report of the Constitutional Reform Commission[9] that was six years in the making, which provides a conscientious overhaul of St. Lucia's constitution, but which Parliament rejected by unanimous vote, is testament to my often-stated tenet that *failure to solve the nation's pressing problems is more a matter of will and desire than a matter of know-how or resources.*

This section highlights some of the Commission's recommendations and suggests how they would transform government into a more inclusive political and economic institution. Following is a summary of these recommendations.

Monarchy to Republican

St. Lucia's monarchical system of government be abolished and replaced with a republican system in which a ceremonial president replaces the monarch as head of state and the pledge of allegiance amended to pay allegiance not to the monarch but to the state of St. Lucia.

Separation of Powers

Except the prime minister and the deputy prime minister, members of the House and the Senate would no longer serve on the Cabinet; a minister selected from Parliament would have to resign from Parliament before joining the Cabinet. When a member of the House is appointed to a ministry, the vacant House seat will be filled by a substitute district representative for the constituency of the departing House member. The Commission's preferred option of executing the replacement of the House member is to require all candidates contesting constituency seats to name a running mate who will then serve as the House replacement if the elected district representative were to take up a Cabinet appointment. However, the Commission referenced a second option — bye-elections in the applicable constituencies to elect substitute House members.

The prime minister, and in his absence the deputy prime minister, would retain the responsibility of appointing ministers, but such ministerial appointments would have to be ratified by Parliament before they come into effect. Bipartisan parliamentary committees to which ministers will be directly accountable will oversee government ministries, departments, agencies, and service commissions. The parliamentary committees will have the power to summon ministers for questioning on the administration, operation, and functioning of their ministries.

Like the prime minister, the deputy prime minister will serve in both Cabinet and Parliament and will be appointed by the president as a member of the House whom the president believes can command the support of the House majority. But unlike the prime minister, the deputy prime minister will have no ministerial authority unless when serving as acting prime minister.

Right of Recall

The constitution be amended to include the right of recall, which is a mechanism to trigger the recall election of a district representative. The right of recall would be automatically launched when an elected House member crosses the floor. And a constituency can initiate a recall if it finds its district representative is in breach of parliamentary ethical standards or code of conduct, or its district representative has, after half a term in office, failed in his or her constituency duties. For a constituency to recall and conduct a by-election to replace its district representative, at least 25 percent of eligible voters must sign a petition for a recall referendum and in the referendum at least 60 percent of eligible voters in the applicable constituency must vote in favor of the recall.

Prime Minister Term Limits and Fixed Date Elections

Prime ministers would not serve for more than three consecutive terms, and parliamentary elections would be held every five years on the 5th anniversary of the previous elections.

Empowering the Senate

Increase the number of senators from 11 to 13, where 7 senators would be appointed by the prime minister, 3 by the minority leader (opposition leader), and 3 by the president. However, a dissenting view of one commissioner (Terrence Charlemagne) was that this recommendation did not go far enough in giving the Senate a greater voice and in improving the balance of power in government. Therefore, an alternative proposal was to increase the number of senators to 15, where the prime minister, the minority leader and the president would each appoint 5 senators.

The Judiciary

The Caribbean Court of Justice should replace the Privy Council as St. Lucia's highest court of appeal. The Eastern Caribbean Supreme Court (ECSC) should remain unchanged. The magistracy should be brought under the full control and management of the Judicial and Legal Services Commission (JLSC). The day-to-day operations of the magistracy should be monitored and managed by a suitable mechanism created within the ECSC and the JLSC. The magistracy should be elevated so it can benefit from the training, independence, mobility, and remuneration enjoyed by the Supreme Court.

Local Government Reform

Local government should be re-instituted and entrenched in the constitution, and should maintain a formal link with the parliamentary representative who would serve as a liaison between local government and central government. Local government authorities should comprise ten members — 2 appointed by the parliamentary representative, 2 by community-based organizations (CBO), and 6 elected in local government elections.

Toward a more Inclusive and Democratic Government

The Commission's recommendation of switching from a monarchical to a republican system of government in which the president replaces the governor general as head of state, and of replacing the Privy Council with the Caribbean Court of Justice as the court of last appeal, might not make a material difference in how the country is governed, but would symbolize the devolution of power to the people, would have the psychological effect of a full and final break from a past that spoke of slavery, colonialism, absolutism and extractive institutions, and would fully realize the democratic notion — government of the people, by the people, for the people.

Perhaps the greatest contributor to St. Lucia's extractive government system is the lack of separation of executive and legislative personnel and functions, and the unfettered power of the prime minister and Cabinet. Thus, the Commission's recommendations on the separation of power would go a long way to fostering a more inclusive political and economic governance system.

The House of Assembly

Excluding elected House members from serving in Cabinet could induce a reduction in parliamentary partisanship since the ruling constituency representatives would feel less compelled to toe the party line now the threat of having their Cabinet position revoked would no longer exist. Reduced emphasis on party line would make the passage of prime ministerial proposals in Parliament a less automatic process, especially when the proposals are controversial, ill-conceived, or ill-advised. For example, in a reformed government, House members may have been more willing to voice their opposition to the DSH agreement, which many view as atrocious to the interest of the country.

Unable to serve in Cabinet, House members are less likely to turn a blind eye to Cabinet corruption of which they would not be direct beneficiaries, and they could devote more time to examining legislation and providing scrutiny and oversight of the executive. House members could likewise devote more time and effort in advocating for and administering to the needs and concerns of their constituencies — i.e., in an ideal world, district representatives would be actively involved in creating economic opportunities for their districts; in the provision, maintenance and proper functioning of such community resources as schools, libraries, ICT centers, roads, and healthcare, and sports, recreation and cultural facilities; and in the preservation and enhancement of their districts' natural and cultural heritage. What obtains in the absence of reform is that contesting and winning a constituency seat seems less about a desire to cater to the needs of the constituency and more about self-aggrandizement and securing a Cabinet ministry with its inherent opportunities for economic extraction.

Former independent senator, Dr. Stephen King,[23] suggested that in a reformed Parliament where elected House members cannot be ministers, constituency representatives' salaries should be set 10 percent higher than that of Cabinet ministers. In the absence of House members doubling as Cabinet ministers, this proposal would provide the financial motivation for attracting quality constituency representative candidates, it would help signal that ministers are subordinate to elected House members to whom they are accountable and answerable, and it is in keeping with the Commission's sentiment that the work of legislatures (especially since they would double as representatives and Cabinet watchdogs) should be a full-time occupation.

One hallmark of true democracy is that power is held in the hands of the people. However, at the present St. Lucians get to exercise that power only on election day. Thereafter, they face what seems like a near absolutist government in which they have little say in government decisions. Parliamentary representatives are supposed to serve as constituency links to government, yet they are often accused of maintaining limited contact with their constituencies and displaying little accountability. The recall election mechanism that aborts the term of a district representative by public vote for misconduct or unsatisfactory performance would return some political power to the people and may induce representatives to dispense their responsibilities in a manner more beneficial to their constituencies.

In terms of accountability, transparency, voter participation, inclusiveness, and government by consensus, Dr. King would like to take matters even further than the recommendations of the Commission. He proposed weekly meetings of representatives with their constituencies; biweekly question-answer meetings of the House of Assembly and the prime minister, to which the public can submit questions; quarterly open Senate forums where the public can submit for Senate debate "motions, private bills, policy documents, or questions"; and quarterly open House of Assembly forums where the public can submit "motions or private bills" for House debate.[23]

The Cabinet

In playing the dual role of executive and legislature and operating in an environment of limited oversight and accountability, Cabinet ministers enjoy undue power. For example, a prime minister cannot easily revoke the Cabinet appointment of an elected House member (say for misconduct or unsatisfactory performance) because the action may incite retaliation in the form of the House member crossing the floor or opposing the prime minister in Parliament. Such political fortification combined with their role as the top-level executor of government policies and programs mean that Cabinet ministers are well positioned to pursue economic extraction. The Commission's separation of power recommendations strip Cabinet ministers of such political power and bring them under the heavy scrutiny and oversight of parliamentary committees vested with political power. Thus, with reform, not only are ministers less able to engage in economic extraction and less likely to get away with incompetence, misconduct, and corruption, but prime ministers can exert greater control over them without fear of political reprisal.

Recent events in government may help illustrate the contrast, in terms of the ability to reprimand ministers, between ministers with the added clout of being elected House members and those without. In 2019, Dr. Ubaldus Raymond,[24] a senator and minister in the ministry of finance, but a non-House member, was forced to resign over private matters that went viral on social media. Though embarrassing and of poor taste, the events were not in violation of any laws, nor did they constitute corruption. In sharp contrast, minister Guy Joseph, an elected member of the House, has repeatedly been involved in scandals that speak of bribery, corruption, and economic extraction, and if factual may constitute criminal offenses, yet, not only is there little chance of his Cabinet appointment being revoked, he grows bolder and more arrogant in government, even to the extent of turning Parliament into a charade, and giving the impression that it is just him and Allen Chastanet running the country.

The Prime Minister

The Commission's recommendations would curb the power of the prime minister in several ways. First, fixed date elections would take away the advantage over opposition parties that prime ministers enjoy in being able to call elections when it best suits their party or when opposition parties are least prepared. Second, by denying prime ministers the possibility of exceeding three terms of unbroken rule, term limits would serve as an interruption in their exercise of power, which is not inconsequential. Consider, for example, the John Compton-led Flambeau Party that ruled St. Lucia for so long (almost 30 years of uninterrupted reign) that most of the country's public institutions, including the police force, were populated with John Compton sympathizers. Thus, according to Rick Wayne, Compton was not just a prime minister. He was an institution. Therefore, any new government would inevitably fail to fully grasp the reins of power because it would come against the Compton institution, which was well poised to undermine its policies and programs, and hence its power. Third, although with Cabinet ministers reduced to a single role, prime ministers would have more control over Cabinet, they would be forced to share that control with House members. For example, ministerial appointments would have to be vetted by parliamentary committees before they come into effect, and parliamentary committees would oversee government ministries and as such have the power to summon ministers for questioning. Fourth, the reforms would induce a more partisan-benign House of Assembly, thus further restraining the powers of prime ministers in that House members would be less willing to rubber-stamp their submissions to Parliament.

The Senate

According to Dr. King[23] the Senate has very little influence on government decisions. He said that during his tenure (2011-2016) as an independent senator, the Senate failed to stop or "significantly influence" not one "motion, resolution or bill" presented to Parliament, including, for example, "the Constituency Council Act, the Anti-Gang Act, the Citizenship by Investment Act, (and) the Constitution Reform Proposals." The Senate's lack of political balance or political independence partly explains its inability to influence government decisions. By constitutional design, the balance of power in the Senate is skewed toward the ruling party, i.e., the prime minister appointments to the Senate constitutes a Senate majority. Thus it is difficult for the Senate to produce the majority votes required to effectively oppose prime minister proposals.

The dissenting view of Terrence Charlemagne, a member of the Constitutional Reform Commission, that the Senate should expand to 15 senators, and the prime minister, minority leader and the president should each appoint an equal number (5) of senators, would broaden political participation, induce greater Senate deliberation, and create a more politically independent Senate that serves less as a rubber stamp of the ruling party and more as an effective check and balance on the powers of the prime minister and the House of Assembly.

Besides the structure of government, partisanship is a significant contributor to the inability to keep governments in check. For any administration, a segment of the population rigorously defends the government regardless of its performance or abuses, while another segment is zealously and overly critical of government. The stalemate that ensues provides the government cover to continue on its merry way. Thus, the Senate moving toward non-partisanship, may help set a healthy tone for the populace and bodes well for democracy.

The Judiciary

The Commission had high praise for the Eastern Caribbean Supreme Court. It reasoned that the fact the Supreme Court was held in high regard in the Caribbean, had many of its decisions upheld by the Privy Council, and had ruled against sitting administrations in several cases, including the St. Lucia Tuxedo scandal, spoke volumes about its independence, veracity, and efficacy. If so, the Supreme Court is well poised to serve as a check and restraint on government overreach and abuse of power. In contrast to the Supreme Court, the Commission found that the integrity, independence, and competency of the magistracy were questionable. However, its recommendations for raising the magistracy to the standards of the Supreme Court would stand it in good stead in serving as a bulwark against the erosion of the rights of citizens, and thus would help strengthen St. Lucia's democracy.

Local Government

In inclusive political institutions, power is broadly distributed. Politically independent local government represents a dispersion of power from the center to the periphery, thus local government symbolizes a more inclusive government system. Local government can also serve as a check and restraint on central government overreach, especially on matters directly pertaining to local jurisdictions. Consider, for example, the Vieux Fort Constituency Council. As an appointed council functioning as an extension of the ruling party, the council has little choice but to rubber-stamp government decisions for its district, DSH being no exception. So much so that the council has been providing the Chastanet administration with cover in that when accused of implementing projects and programs in Vieux Fort with no public consultation, the administration's patented response is that the council was consulted, which is a disingenuous reaction since as a politically appointed body, the council is not representative of the district and cannot provide the government with effective opposition. The story changes completely, if, under the recommendations of the Commission, the council was an independent local government authority, one with jurisdiction over its land-use planning, it could have provided significant opposition to the DSH initiative and any other initiatives deemed inimical to the interest of the district. Therefore, local government does not only help induce political inclusiveness; it helps increase political participation and community empowerment; and it helps in the balancing of power and in the solidification of democracy.

Regulatory Instruments

In attempting to foster a more responsive, participatory, accountable, representative government devoid of abuse of power and economic extraction, the Commission did not stop at the separation and balancing of power and the restructuring of government. It reviewed and made recommendations on strengthening regulatory institutions and instruments that provide scrutiny and oversight geared toward keeping government in check. These included Parliamentary Commissioner, Integrity Commission, Public Accounts Committee, Contractor-General, and Campaign Finance regulation.

Parliamentary Commissioner. Enshrined in the constitution, the Parliamentary Commissioner is charged with the investigation of injury or injustice complaints arising from a fault in government administration. This provision helps safeguard citizens from inadvertent maladministration, political victimization, and the malfeasance of public officials. To improve the effectiveness, prominence, visibility, and financial independence of the Parliamentary Commissioner, the Commission recommended that Parliamentary Commissioner reports be released verbatim to the public; the House of Assembly appoint a select committee to review these reports and ensure their recommendations are implemented; and measures be adopted guaranteeing the Parliamentary Commissioner's efficacy and financial independence.

Integrity Commission. The Integrity Commission was established under the Integrity in Public Life Act to promote good governance and to eliminate corruption in public life. The Act mandates constituency representatives, senior public servants, and persons managing statutory corporations to file declaration of income, assets, and liabilities with the Integrity Commission. The Constitutional Reform Commission recommended expanding the list of persons and public entities falling under the scrutiny of the Integrity Commission; imposing sanctions on persons or entities failing to comply with the Act; and requiring all members of Parliament and Cabinet to file a declaration within 30 days of taking office.

Public Accounts Committee. Established by a standing order of the House of Assembly, the Public Accounts Committee is a bipartisan Parliament select committee duty-bound to scrutinize government appropriation accounts and the report of the Director of Audit on these accounts. The Committee examines government revenue and expenditure to ascertain their efficacy and veracity and to promote transparency and accountability in the financial dealings of government. The Commission recommended that the Public Accounts Committee be entrenched in the constitution and established as a joint select committee of Parliament with an expanded membership to include persons with accounting and other requisite skills. It also recommended that the Public Accounts Committee should have the power to request independent audits and to investigate the finances of entities regardless of whether they have submitted an audit report; and it should impose disciplinary action against persons or entities failing to comply with its requests.

Contractor General. As discussed above, public contracts have presented politicians with one of the greatest opportunities for economic extraction. The office of the contractor general was created specifically to help curb corruption in the public procurement of goods and services. The contractor general monitors the award and implementation of public contracts to ensure contracts are awarded or terminated in accordance with best practice and are implemented in conformity with agreed-upon terms of reference; and to investigate fraud, corruption, mismanagement, waste or abuse in the awarding and implementation of contracts. The Commission recommended that the office of Contractor General be included in the constitution and have jurisdiction over government ministries, departments, and agencies; local government authorities; statutory bodies and authorities; and any establishment in which government or an agency of government owns at least 51 percent of its shares.

Campaign Finance Reform. The Commission recommended the enactment of a Political Party and Elections Campaign Finance Act to safeguard the integrity of the nation's democracy by promoting a fair and equitable electoral process and preventing the capture of the State by criminal, foreign, and commercial interest. The Act would require political parties to declare their assets and liabilities and provide full disclosure of their campaign financial contributions. The Act would ban election financial contributions to political parties from all anonymous sources, foreign countries, and foreign companies; and would place a limit on the amount companies and individuals can contribute to political parties and on the level of contributions that would not require declaration. The Act would stipulate sanctions to impose on political parties in violation of its provisions, and would require that the government fund all political parties and engender them to have equal access to State media.

Summary

In summary, the proposed constitutional and government reforms would help check and restrain the power of government and make government more accountable to voters. The recall election mechanism along with precluding House members from serving in Cabinet would curb the powers of constituency representatives, induce them to be more accountable to their constituencies and more responsive to their needs and concerns, and enable them to provide Cabinet with greater scrutiny and oversight. Disallowing Cabinet ministers to serve as parliamentarians and subjecting them to the intense scrutiny and oversight of nonpartisan parliamentary committees, thus forcing them to be more accountable to the legislature, would serve as a check and restraint on the powers of Cabinet, and would reduce the dominance of the executive over the legislature. Likewise, prime minister term limits, fixed date general elections, a House of Assembly over which a prime minister can exert limited control, and a balance of power less skewed toward the executive branch would help curb the powers of the prime minister.

The reforms aimed at strengthening the institutions and processes of scrutiny and oversight would help promote good governance, protect citizens against government maladministration and malfeasance, help eliminate corruption in public life and in the award and implementation of public contracts, ensure government financial dealings are transparent and can stand up to scrutiny, and protect the integrity of the democracy and political system by preventing state capture and promoting electoral fairness and equity.

Therefore, with these reforms, the country stands a better chance of avoiding the excesses, abuse of power, mismanagement, and economic extraction observed in previous administrations. Hence the stance that constitutional reform and not the removal of Chastanet from government is the most critical issue facing the country. If so, in this coming election the Labour Party would do well to place constitutional reform firmly on its platform agenda and seek the mandate of three-fourth House majority needed to enact constitutional reform.

Allen Michael Chastanet
(born November 20, 1960)

Prime minister of St. Lucia since June 2016.

NOTES / REFERENCES

Chapter 1: By Hook or by Crook

1. Lansiquot, P. (2020, June 13). Open letter to prime minister of St Lucia. *Caribbean News Global (CNG)*. Retrieved from https://www.caribbeannewsglobal.com/open-letter-to-prime-minister-of-st-lucia/

2. Prescod, D. (2018, May 19). Time to Resign! Part 2. *The Voice*. Retrieved from https://www.thevoiceslu.com/2018/05/time-to-resign-part-2/

3. Reynolds, A. (2005, Winter). St. Lucia's men of the century. *The Jako*. Retrieved from http://www.jakoproductions.com/society/MenofTheCentury.pdf.

4. Reynolds, A. and Lansiquot, P. (forthcoming, 2021). *They Call Him Brother George: Portrait of a Caribbean Politician*. Vieux Fort, St. Lucia: Jako Books.

5. George, M. (2020, January 4). Former Senator/Minister Regrets Supporting CIP. *The Voice*. Retrieved from https://www.thevoiceslu.com/2020/01/former-senator-minister-regrets-supporting-cip/

6. Reynolds, A. (2007). The Pearl of the Caribbean. *The Voice*. Retrieved from http://www.jakoproductions.com/society/ThePearlofTheCaribbean.pdf

7. Prescott, S.L. (2019, October 9). DSH-Horse Race Track: Our Gift to Teo Ah King. *Caribbean News Global*. Retrieved from https://www.caribbeannewsglobal.com/desert-star-holdings-horse-racetrack-st-lucias-gift-to-teo-ah-king/

8. James, J. (2018, February 15). DSH Project — A Hasty, High-Handed, Horrendous Deal of Exclusion. *The Voice*. Retrieved from https://www.thevoiceslu.com/2018/02/dsh-project-hasty-high-handed-horrendous-deal-exclusion/

9. Kelly, S. (2017, August 7). St Lucia government must stop 'silence' on DSH – Hilaire. *WIC News*. Retrieved from https://wicnews.com/caribbean/st-lucia-government-must-stop-silence-on-dsh-hilaire-16034287/

10. *Vieux Fort*. (2020). Retrieved from https://www.jakoproductions.com/vieux-fort/

11. One Saint Lucia. (2020). *A development agenda for Saint Lucia*. Retrieved from http://www.oursaintlucia.com/

12. Prescod, D. (2017, September 23). Our economy – Part 1: A good dose of 'Chini Twèf'. *The Voice*. Retrieved from https://www.thevoiceslu.com/2017/09/economy-part-1-good-dose-chini-twef/

13. Prescod, D. (2017, September 30). Our Economy — Part 2: Digging a deeper grave. *The Voice*. Retrieved from https://www.thevoiceslu.com/2017/09/economy-part-2-digging-deeper-grave/

14. Prescod, D. (2017, October 7). Our Economy – Part 3: The private sector conundrum. *The Voice*. Retrieved from https://www.thevoiceslu.com/2017/10/economy-part-3-private-sector-conundrum/

Chapter 2: The Crux of the Matter

1. Wayne, R. (2017, April 8). New Law Resurrects Rochamel Controversy! *The Star*. Retrieved from https://stluciastar.com/new-law-resurrects-rochamel-controversy/

2. Micah George, M. (2017, December 30). The Grynberg/St. Lucia matter – an inside look. *The Voice*. Retrieved from https://www.thevoiceslu.com/2017/12/grynberg-st-lucia-matter-inside-look/

3. St. Lucia Government Information Service. (2014, December 15). *St. Lucia News Online*. Retrieved from https://www.stlucianewsonline.com/government-seeks-investors-for-le-paradis/

4. Government of St. Lucia. (2016). *DSH Framework and Supplementary Agreements*. Retrieved from http://www.jakoproductions.com/vieuxfort/DSHAgreements.pdf

5. DSH Caribbean Star Ltd. (2016, January 19). *Master plan presentation: Integrated Resort Development, Vieux Fort, St. Lucia*. Retrieved from http://www.jakoproductions.com/vieuxfort/DSHLabor.pdf

6. Desert Star Holdings Limited (DSH). (2019). *Pearl of the Caribbean*. Retrieved from https://desertstargroup.com/desert-star-holdings-limited-description/

7. Acemoglu, D. & Robinson J.D. (2012). *Why Nations Fail: The Origins of Power, Prosperity, and Poverty*. New York: Currency.

8. Government of Saint Lucia. (2011). *Report of the Saint Lucia Constitutional Reform Commission*. Retrieved from http://www.govt.lc/publications/report-of-the-saint-lucia-constitutional-reform-commission

9. King, S. (2020, June 10). Enough is enough. *Caribbean News Global*. Retrieved from https://www.caribbeannewsglobal.com/enough-is-enough/

10. KnowledgeWalk Institute. (2019). *Caribbean elections: St. Lucia Election Centre 2016* (election results 1951 - 2016). Retrieved from http://caribbeanelections.com/lc/elections/

11. Wayne, R. (2020, March 14). Constitutional reform: Crossing the floor and The Right of Recall! *The Star*. Retrieved from https://stluciastar.com/constitutional-reform-crossing-the-floor-and-the-right-of-recall/

12. George, M. (2020, June 15). RSLPF says no permission was sought for Sunday's motorcade. *The Voice*. Retrieved from https://www.thevoiceslu.com/2020/06/rslpf-says-no-permission-was-sought-for-sundays-motorcade/

13. Mc Donald, N. (2011, September 25). Richard Frederick Resigns! *The Star*. Retrieved from https://stluciastar.com/richard-frederick-resigns/

14. A Hail Mary for Francis of St. Lucia! (2015, April 25). *The Star*. Retrieved from https://stluciastar.com/a-hail-mary-for-francis-of-st-lucia/

15. Antoine, A. (2020, July 2). *Facebook conversation with Andrew Antoine*. Retrieved from https://www.facebook.com/groups/282803341756900/permalink/3052562134780993

Chapter 3: An Intriguing Question

1. The World Bank. (2019). *Life expectancy at birth*. Retrieved from https://data.worldbank.org/indicator/SP.DYN.LE00.IN?end=2016 &locations=LC&start=1960

2. Central Statistics Office, Government of St. Lucia. (2010). *St Lucia 2010 Population and Housing Census*. Castries, St. Lucia.

3. United States Central Intelligence Agency (CIA). (2020). *The World Fact Book*. Retrieved from https://www.cia.gov/library/publications/the-world-factbook/geos/st.html

4. Wikipedia. (2020). *Demographics of Saint Lucia*. Retrieved from https://en.wikipedia.org/wiki/Demographics_of_Saint_Lucia

Chapter 4: A Question of Fitness

1. KnowledgeWalk Institute. (2020). *Biography: Allen Chastanet*. Retrieved from http://www.caribbeanelections.com/knowledge/biography/bios/chastanet_allen.asp.

2. Government of St. Lucia. (2012). *Senator the Honourable Allen M. Chastanet*. Retrieved from https://archive.stlucia.gov.lc/govfolks/sen_the_hon_allen_chastanet.htm

3. Joseph, T. (2016, May 24). All ah we is one: Chastanet's test. *NationNews*. Retreived from https://www.nationnews.com/nationnews/news/81571/ah-chastanet-test

4. Chastanet, M. (2016). *Room at the top: The Story of a ninth born who became #1*. Gros Islet, St. Lucia: Star Publishing.

5. Hall, D. (1982). *The Caribbean experience: An historical survey 1450-1960* (pp. 53). Kingston Jamaica; Port of Spain, Trinidad & Tobago: Heinemann Educational Books.

6. *Prime Minister Allen Chastanet: "I am a product of Canada."* Available from https://www.youtube.com/watch?v=4Ltma8a-UEM

Chapter 5: The Cream Shall Rise

1. KnowledgeWalk Institute. (2020). *Biography: Vaughan Allen Lewis.* Retrieved from http://caribelect.easycgi.com/knowledge/biography/bios/lewis_vaughan.asp

2. A Hail Mary for Francis of St. Lucia! (2015, April 25). *The Star.* Retrieved from https://stluciastar.com/a-hail-mary-for-francis-of-st-lucia/

3. Ellis, G. (2007, May 2). Tiny St. Lucia earns a big enemy: China. *The Seattle Times.* Retrieved from https://www.seattletimes.com/nation-world/tiny-st-lucia-earns-a-big-enemy-china/

4. Sir John Compton his last days. (2007, September 11). *The Voice,* pp. 7.

5. Blood on their hands. (2007, September 22). *Crusader,* pp. 2-3.

6. KnowledgeWalk Institute. (2020). *Biograpy: Stephenson King.* Retrieved from http://www.caribbeanelections.com/knowledge/biography/bios/king_stephenson.asp

7. Wayne, R. (2017, April 22). Federick versus government: Judge delivers shock verdict! *The Star.* Retrieved from https://stluciastar.com/federick-versus-government-judge-delivers-shock-verdict/

8. Wayne, R. (2007, August 11). Could a murderer be St. Lucia's next prime minister? *The Star.*

9. Frederick, V. (2007, August 16). Rufus Bousquet comes clean: "I am Bruce Duane Tucker!" *The Star.*

10. Mc Donald, N. (2011, September 21). PM turns to Washington on Visa Revocation. *The Star.* Retrieved from https://stluciastar.com/pm-turns-to-washington-on-visa-revocation/

11. Tom Chou to return? (2016, June 13). *St. Lucia Times.* Retrieved from https://stluciatimes.com/tom-chou-return/

12. Mc Donald, N. (2011, September 25). Richard Frederick Resigns! *The Star.* Retrieved from https://stluciastar.com/richard-frederick-resigns/

Chapter 6: Against All Odds

1. Alphonse, M. (2016, June 3). Commentary: Polls, VAT and flawed manifestos mire St Lucia election. *Caribbean News Now*. Retrieved from https://www.stlucianewsonline.com/polls-vat-and-flawed-manifestos-mire-st-lucia-election-commentary/

2. Lee, J.A. (Producer/Presenter). (2019, February 22). *Sir John: In his own words*. St. Lucia Government Information Service and office of the Prime Minister in association with National Archives Authority of St. Lucia, and AnCom Ltd. Avialable from https//youtu.be/Umq5atRrvRm

3. Greene, R. and Elffers, J. (2000). *The 48 Laws of Power*. New York: Penguin Books.

4. Chastanet, M. (2016). *Room at the top: The story of a ninth born who became #1*. Castries: Star Publishing.

5. Reynolds, A. (2005, Winter). St. Lucia Men of the Century: Sir George Charles, Sir John Compton and George Odlum. *The Jako*. Retrieved from http://www.jakoproductions.com/society/MenofThe-Century.pdf

6. Reynolds, A. (2005, Spring). St. Lucia Men of the Century: Sir George Charles, Sir John Compton and George Odlum (Part II). *The Jako*. Retrieved from http://www.jakoproductions.com/society/MenofTheCentury.pdf

7. Fevrier, M. (Interviewer). (2018, December 5). *What's up Doc? Up Close & Personal with Dr. Kenny Anthony*. MBC Television Saint Lucia. Available from https://www.facebook.com/mbcslu/videos/2794162757264333/

8. Charles, G. F. L. (1994). *The history of the labour movement in St. Lucia, 1945-1974*. Castries, St. Lucia: Folk Research Centre Historical Perspective Series.

9. Harmsen, J., Ellis, G., and Devaux, R. (2012). *A History of St. Lucia*. Cape Moule A Chique, Vieux Fort, St. Lucia: Light House Road Publications.

10. Government of St. Lucia, Central Statistics Office. (2020). *2010 Population and Housing Census – Preliminary Report*. Retrieved from https://www.stats.gov.lc/wp-content/uploads/2016/12/StLuci-aPreliminaryCensusReport2010.pdf

11. KnowledgeWalk Institute. (2019). *Caribbean Elections: St. Lucia Election Centre 2016 (Election Results 1951 - 2016)*. Retrieved from http://caribbeanelections.com/lc/elections/

12. Reynolds, A. (2005, Summer/Fall). The Life & Art of Dunstan St. Omer. *The Jako*, pp. 28-47. Retrieved from http://www.jakoproductions.com/culture/DunstanSaintOmer.pdf

13. Reynolds, A. (2003). *The Struggle for Survival: An historical, political, and socioeconomic perspective of St. Lucia* (Third Edition). Vieux Fort St. Lucia: Jako Books.

14. Reynolds, A. (2015, March 31). The Exploitation of Vieux Fort. *The Voice*. Retrieved from https://www.thevoiceslu.com/2015/03/the-exploitation-of-vieux-fort/

15. Mayers, G. (2016, March 26). IMPACS – Dr. Anthony must account. *The Voice*. Retrieved from https://www.thevoiceslu.com/2016/03/impacs-dr-anthony-must-account/

16. Impacts From IMPACS. (2015, March 19). *The Voice*. Retrieved from https://www.thevoiceslu.com/2015/03/impacts-from-impacs/

17. IMPACS Report: Who's saying what? (2015, March 14). *The Star*. Retrieved from https://stluciastar.com/impacs-report-who-is-saying-what/

18. Untold Stories. (2017, October 28). *The St. Jude reconstruction project documentary part 2*. Retrieved from https://youtu.be/MdRO8q_TyR8

19. Mondesir: Current St. Judes Hospital location a "dungeon of shame". (2017, September 12). *St. Lucia Times*. Retrieved from https://stluciatimes.com/mondesir-current-sjh-location-dungeon-shame/

20. Wikipedia. (2019). *Walid Juffali*. Retrieved from https://en.wikipedia.org/wiki/Walid_Juffali#mw-head

21. Office of the Prime Minister. (2015). *Statement on Dr. Walid Juffali*. Retrieved from http://education.govt.lc/news/statement-on-dr-walid-juffali

22. June 6 election day. (2016, May 19). *The Voice*. Retrieved from https://www.thevoiceslu.com/2016/05/june-6-election-day/

Chapter 7: It's All About Culture

1. Lansiquot, P. (2020, June 13). Open letter to prime minister of St Lucia. *Caribbean News Global (CNG)*. Retrieved from https://www.caribbeannewsglobal.com/open-letter-to-prime-minister-of-st-lucia/

2. Pierre Criticises Chastanet Over Statement About Colonialism, Economics, (2020, May 21). *St. Lucia Times*. Retrieved from https://stluciatimes.com/pierre-criticises-chastanet-over-statement-about-colonialism-economics/

3. Lee, J.A. (Producer/Presenter). (2004, February 14). *Sir John: In his own words*. St. Lucia Government Information Service and office of the Prime Minister in association with National Archives Authority of St. Lucia, and AnCom Ltd. Avialable from https//youtu.be/Umq5atRrvRm

4. Huntington, S.P. (1996).*The clash of civilizations and the remaking of world order*. New York: Simon & Schuster.

5. Mottley, M.A. (2020, October 26). *IDB pivot – keynote*. Retrieved from https://www.youtube.com/watch?v=_l_y2fB-l_0

6. Naipaul, V.S. (1962). *The middle passage*. London: Vintage Books.

Chapter 8: Putting Foreigners First

1. Government of St. Lucia. (2016). *DSH Framework and Supplementary Agreements*. Retrieved from http://www.jakoproductions.com/vieuxfort/DSHAgreements.pdf.

2. YIM, B. (2019). Discover a rare pearl. *MILLIONAIREASIA*. Retrieved from https://millionaireasia.com/wp-content/uploads/2019/07/POC_TeoAhKhing_6pp_R4.pdf

3. Reynolds, A. (2017). *The pearl of the Caribbean*. Retrieved from http://www.jakoproductions.com/society/ThePearlofThe-Caribbean.pdf

4. AI Training and Call Center to Open in Vieux Fort. (2017, March 17). *The Voice*. Retrieved from https://www.thevoiceslu.com/2017/03/ai-training-call-center-open-vieux-fort/

5. McDonald, N. (2018, February 3). *Progress report: OJO Labs makes Saint Lucia a Caribbean Leader in New Technology.* Retrieved from https://stluciastar.com/progress-report-ojo-labs-makes-saint-lucia-caribbean-leader-new-technology/

6. Government of St. Lucia, Central Statistical Office. (2020). *Labour Force.* Retrieved from https://www.stats.gov.lc/subjects/society/labour-force/

7. Eliza Victor, E. (2017, May 11). Castries South MP calls out Cabinet on foreign investor concessions. *GVD News.* Available from https://www.youtube.com/watch?v=vl0zbzgtPKo

8. Cabot St Lucia golf resort explained – Part 1. (2020, February 11). *Caribbean News Global (CNG).* Retrieved from https://www.caribbeannewsglobal.com/cabot-st-lucia-golf-resort-explained-part-1/

9. Cabot St Lucia golf resort explained – Part 2. (2020, February 13). *Caribbean News Global (CNG).* Retrieved from https://www.caribbeannewsglobal.com/cabot-st-lucia-golf-resort-explained-part-2/

10. Government of St. Lucia. (2005). *CHAPTER 16.01: National Insurance Corporation Act.* Retrieved from ACThttps://stlucianic.org/downloadarea/nicact.pdf

11. Cabot St Lucia golf resort explained ... 'That's by Design' (2020, February 10). *Caribbean News Global (CNG).* Retrieved from https://www.caribbeannewsglobal.com/cabot-st-lucia-golf-resort-explained-thats-by-design/

Chapter 9: Putting St. Lucians Last

1. Kairi Consultants. (2018). *Saint Lucia national Report of living conditions 2016.* OECS Commission. Retrieved from https://www.stats.gov.lc/wp-content/uploads/2019/01/Saint-Lucia-National-Report-of-Living-Conditions-2016-Final_December-2018.pdf

2. Staff Reporter. (2019, April 24). People's Distress Fund Launched to Help Fire Victims. *Loop.* Retrieved from http://www.loopslu.com/content/peoples-distress-fund-launched-help-fire-victims

3. Reffes, M. (2017, July 12). The Caribbean's top music festivals. *USA Today*. Retrieved from https://www.usatoday.com/story/travel/experience/caribbean/2017/07/12/music-festivals-caribbean/468046001/

4. Seon, E. (2017, May 8). Prime Minister Chastanet confirms cut in subvention to St. Lucia National Trust. *Caribbean Times*. Retrieved from https://caribbeantimesnyc.com/2017/05/prime-minister-chastanet-confirms-cut-in-subvention-to-st-lucia-national-trust/

5. Tulsie, B. (2017, April 25). National Trust Issues Statement on Subvention Cut. *The Voice*. Retrieved from https://www.thevoiceslu.com/2017/04/national-trust-issues-statement-subvention-cut/

6. Reynolds, A. (2003). *The Struggle for Survival: An historical, political, and socioeconomic perspective of St. Lucia* (Third Edition, pp. 170-205). Vieux Fort St. Lucia: Jako Books.

7. Dart, T. (2017, June 21). Derek Walcott museum closes amid row over Caribbean tourist developments. *The Guardian*. Retrieved from https://www.theguardian.com/books/2017/jun/21/derek-walcott-museum-st-lucia-caribbean-tourism#

8. St. Lucia National Trust. (2017, May 31). Press Release: St. Lucia National Trust to close Walcott House due to funding cuts. *St. Lucia News Online*. https://www.stlucianewsonline.com/press-release-walcott-place-to-close/

9. George, M. (2017, May 13). RSL to close, Union to meet employees. *The Voice*. https://www.thevoiceslu.com/2017/05/rsl-close-union-meet-employees/

10. Mc Dowell, C.E. (2017, January 30). Jamaica Kincaid Revisits 'The Star Apple Kingdom' at Walcott Lecture. *The Star*. https://stluciastar.com/jamaica-kincaid-revisits-star-apple-kingdom-walcott-lecture/

11. Reynolds, A. (2005, Summer/Fall). The Making of ECTEL: A lesson in Caribbean integration (Part I). *The Jako*, pp. 8-20. Retrieved from http://www.jakoproductions.com/culture/Summer/Fall2005.pdf

12. Cental Intellegence Agency (CIA). (2020). *The World Factbook*. Retrieved from https://www.cia.gov/library/publications/the-world-factbook/geos/st.html

13. Chastanet, A. (2013, August 7). *Allen Chastanet U.W.P political leader address to the nation*. Retrieved from https://www.slideshare.net/unitedpacsaintlucia/ac-address-to-the-nation

14. Government of St Lucia deprives 8,000 students one-laptop-per child programme. (2020, February 18). *Caribbean Global News (CNG)*. Retrieved from https://www.caribbeannewsglobal.com/government-of-st-lucia-deprives-8000-students-one-laptop-per-child-programme/

15. Cunningham, J.M. (2020). *Did Marie-Antoinette Really Say "Let Them Eat Cake"?* Encyclopædia Britannica. Retrieved from https://www.britannica.com/story/did-marie-antoinette-really-say-let-them-eat-cake

16. Dantes, S.A. (2020, April 22). The reality of laptops for students in St. Lucia. *The Voice*. https://www.thevoiceslu.com/2020/04/the-reality-of-laptops-for-students-in-saint-lucia/

Chapter 10: Disregard for the Laws of the Land

1. Minister revokes appointments of NURC commissioners. (2018, July 20). *St. Lucia News Online*. Retrieved from https://www.stlucianewsonline.com/minister-revokes-appointments-of-nurc-

2. Government of St. Lucia. (2016). *National Utilities Regulatory Commission Act*. Retrieved from http://nurc.org.lc/wp-content/uploads/2017/11/National-Utilities-Regulatory-Commission-Act-No-3-of-2016-005-003.pdf

3. National Trust. (May 26, 2020). *Government reneges on commitment to protect historic building*. Retrieved from https://www.slyoumag.com/2020/05/26/national-trust-government-reneges-on-commitment-to-protect-historic-building/

4. St. Lucia National Trust. (2020, March 12). Massive bulldozing ongoing - Artifacts found - Agencies take action. *Change.org*. Retrieved from https://www.change.org/p/government-of-saint-lucia-maintain-local-rights-and-promote-sustainable-development-save-our-coast/u/25900221

5. Jannine Compton-Antoine, J. (2020). *Choice News Now Prime Special Report*. Choice TV.

6. National Trust. (2020, August 12). National Trust urges government to reconsider decision to lease Queen's Chain to Cabot Saint Lucia for 75 years. *The Star*. Retrieved from https://stluciastar.com/national-trust-urges-government-to-reconsider-decision-to-lease-queens-chain-to-cabot-saint-lucia-for-75-years/

7. Hennecart, M. (2018, November 11). *Stretching Saint Lucia beyond her limit: the Queen's Chain, a spatial injustice issue!* Retrieved from https://www.facebook.com/notes/mark-hennecart/stretching-saint-lucia-beyond-her-limit-the-queens-chain-a-spatial-injustice-iss/10156429075810845/

9. Williams, B. (2011, February 14). The Queen's Chain and our survival. *The Star*. Retrieved from https://stluciastar.com/the-queens-chain-and-the-strict-laws-of-survival-for-us/

9. Government of St. Lucia. (2016). *Chapter 5.12: Physical planning and development act*. Retrieved from https://observatoriop10.cepal.org/sites/default/files/documents/physical-planning-and-development-act-cap-5.12.pdf

10. Untold Stories. (2017, October 28). *The St. Jude reconstruction project documentary part 2*. Retrieved from https://youtu.be/MdRO8q_TyR8

Chapter 11: Modus Operandi

1. Governent of St. Lucia. (2020, July 27). *Fiscal Incentives (Fresh Start Construction Company Limited) Order*: Statutory Instrument 2020. No. 119.

2. *Fresh start incentives raise eyebrows*. (2020, July 30). HTS News4orce St. Lucia. Obtained from https://youtu.be/i-KwgFpImuM

3. George, M. (2019, May 21). Economic Development Minister Guy Joseph Calls Pierre "A Fool" Over PAJOAH Letter. *The Voice*. Retrieved from https://www.thevoiceslu.com/2019/05/economic-development-minister-guy-joseph-calls-pierre-a-fool-over-pajoah-lette/

4. Pierre, P.J. (2019, May 30). Pierre: Guy Joseph's Response In PJOAH Letter Scandal An Insult To All Saint Lucians. *St. Lucia Times*. Retrieved from https://stluciatimes.com/pierre-guy-josephs-response-in-pjoah-letter-scandal-an-insult-to-all-saint-lucians/

5. PAJOAH letter scandal: symptom of corruption in St Lucia. (2019, June 12). *MENAFN*. Retrieved from https://menafn.com/1098637808/PAJOAH-letter-scandal-symptom-of-corruption-in-St-Lucia 1/

6. Kaplan, A. and Leibowitz A. (2018, September 3). A South Florida businessman wanted to rebuild a Caribbean airport. How things got bungled. *Miami Herald*. Retrieved from https://www.miamiherald.com/

7. *St Lucia minister called on to answer bribery allegations*. (n.d.). The Caribbean Radio. Retrieved from https://www.thecaribbeanradio.com/st-lucia-minister-called-on-to-answer-bribery-allegations/

8. Frederick, R. (2017, May 4). *St. Lucia Airport Bribes*. MBC. Obtained from https://youtu.be/R450aHJQ4Oo.

9. Saint Lucia airport corruption allegations attract US media attention. (2018, September 4). *St. Lucia News Online*. Retrieved from https://www.stlucianewsonline.com/saint-lucia-airport-corruption-allegations-attract-us-media-attention/

10. Nestor, D. (2018, February 20). Guy Joseph: "They Paid $3 Million to Investigate Me" *The Voice*. Retrieved from https://www.thevoiceslu.com/2018/02/guy-joseph-paid-3-million-investigate/

11. George, M. (2019, September 14). EC$534 million for HIA redevelopment--government says no to PPP for HIA. *The Voice*. Retrieved from https://www.thevoiceslu.com/2019/09/ec534-million-for-hia-redevelopment-government-says-no-to-ppp-for-hia/

12. Pierre, P.J. (2019, March 20). SLP leader says government callous, insensitive regarding health care. *St. Lucia Times*. Retrieved from https://stluciatimes.com/slp-leader-says-government-callous-insensitive-regarding-health-care/

13. State of Urgency 2020. (2020). *State of Urgency online poll*. Conducted August/September 2020 by Lyndale James and Jimmy Fletcher to gain insights into how St. Lucians view the socio-political environment in the country.

Chapter 12: It's the Economy, Stupid

1. The Central Statistical Office of Saint Lucia. (2020). *Unemployment rate (overall)*. Retrieved from https://www.stats.gov.lc/

2. The World Bank. (2020). *Unemployment, total (% of total labor force) - St. Lucia*. Retrieved from https://data.worldbank.org/indicator/SL.UEM.TOTL.ZS?locations=LC

3. The World Bank. (2020). *GDP growth (annual %) - St. Lucia*. Retrieved from https://data.worldbank.org/indicator/NY.GDP.MKTP.KD.ZG?locations=LC

4. IndexMundi (2019). *Saint Lucia public debt*. Retrieved from https://www.indexmundi.com/saint_lucia/public_debt.html

5. Macrotrends (2020). *St. Lucia Murder/Homicide Rate 1990-2020*. Retrieved from https://www.macrotrends.net/countries/LCA/st-lucia/murder-homicide-rate

Chapter 13: The Compton Deficiency

1. Cental Intellegence Agency (CIA). (2020). *The World Factbook*. Retrieved from https://www.cia.gov/library/publications/the-world-factbook/geos/st.html

2. Harmsen, J. (2020, June 26). *Conversation with Jolien Harmsen*. Obtained from email correspondence.

3. Wayne, R. (2007, September). *Like it or lump it, John Compton is indisputably St. Lucia's Man of the century!* (pp. 8, 10, 12,). A special supplement in honor of Sir Compton. Castires, St. Lucia: Star Publishing.

4. Reynolds, A. (2003). *The struggle for survival: an historical, political and socioeconomic perspective of St. Lucia* (pp. 170-205). Vieux Fort, St. Lucia: Jako Books.

5. Charles, G.F.L. (1994). *The History of the labor movement in St. Lucia – 1945-1974: A personal memoir* (pp.39). Castires, St. Lucia: Folk Research Center.

6. Charles, G.F.L. (1994). *The History of the labor movement in St. Lucia – 1945-1974: A personal memoir* (pp.56). Castries, St. Lucia: Folk Research Center.

7. Charles, G.F.L. (1994). *The History of the labor movement in St. Lucia – 1945-1974: A personal memoir* (pp.48). Castries, St. Lucia: Folk Research Center. Revolvers

8. Lee, J.A. (Producer/Presenter). (2004, February 14). *Sir John: In his own words.* St. Lucia Government Information Service and office of the Prime Minister in association with National Archives Authority of St. Lucia, and AnCom Ltd. Avialable from https//youtu.be/Umq5atRrvRm

9. Odlum, G. (1993). *The moral agenda: Crusader editorials of the year – 1993* (pp. 29-30). Castries, St. Lucia: The Crusader.

Chapter 14: A Political Leadership Crisis

1. St. Rose, A. (2020, August 17). Choiseul – Saltibus regains its independence with Dr. St Rose. *Caribbean News Global.* Retrieved from https://www.caribbeannewsglobal.com/choiseul-saltibus-regains-its-independence-with-dr-st-rose/

2. Pierre, P.J. (2020, July 15). SLP statement on candidate selection says no individual bigger than the party. *St. Lucia Times.* Retrieved from https://stluciatimes.com/slp-statement-on-candidate-selection-says-no-individual-bigger-than-the-party/

3. Andrews, M. (n.d.). *Vieux Fort: Yesterday, today and tomorrow.* Retrieved from https://www.jakoproductions.com/vieux-fort-yesterday-today-tomorrow-marcus-andrews/

4. Harmsen, J. (1999). *Sugar, slavery and settlement: A social history of Vieux Fort, St. Lucia, from the Amerindians to the present.* Castries, St. Lucia: St. Lucia National Trust.

5. KnowledgeWalk Institute. (2019). *Caribbean Elections: Election Results 1951 - 2016.* Retrieved from http://www.caribbeanelections.com/lc/elections/

6. Wayne, R. (1977). *It'll be alright in the morning.* Castries, St. Lucia: Star Publishing.

7. Wayne, R. (1986). *Foolish Virgins.* Castries, St. Lucia: Star Publishing.

8. Reynolds, A. (2017). *The Stall Keeper* (pp. 45-47). Vieux Fort, St. Lucia: Jako Books

9. Kairi Consultants. (2018). *Saint Lucia national report of living conditions 2016.* Retrieved from https://www.stats.gov.lc/wp-content/uploads/2019/01/Saint-Lucia-National-Report-of-Living-Conditions-2016-Final_December-2018.pdf

10. Government of St. Lucia, Central Statistical Office. (2020). *Unemployment rates by district and sex, 2010 to 2019.* Retrieved from https://www.stats.gov.lc/subjects/society/labour-force/

Chapter 15: Persistent Unemployment

1. KnowledgeWalk Institute. (2019). *Saint Lucia Labour Party: Our Blue Print for Growth.* Retrieved from http://www.caribbeanelections.com/eDocs/manifestos/lc/SLP_manifesto_2011.pdf

2. Wayne, K. (2011, October 10). King's $300 million stimulus package! *The Star.* Retrieved from https://stluciastar.com/king%E2%80%99s-300-million-stimulus-package/

3. Governement of St. Lucia, Office of the Prime minister. (2014, December 2). *Employment initiative gets boost.* Retrieved from http://www.govt.lc/news/employment-initiative-gets-boost

4. UN Office for the Coordination of Humanitarian Affairs (OCHA). (2020). *Saint Lucia country profile as of July 2020.* Retrieved from https://www.humanitarianresponse.info/en/operations/latin-america-and-caribbean/document/st-lucia-country-profile-july-2020

5. The Central Statistical Office of Saint Lucia. (2020). *Unemployment rate (overall).* Retrieved from https://www.stats.gov.lc/

6. The World Bank. (2020). *GDP growth (annual %) - St. Lucia.* Retrieved from https://data.worldbank.org/indicator/NY.GDP.MKTP.KD.ZG?locations=LC

7. Government of St. Lucia, Central Statistical Office. (2020). *Unemployed labour force.* Retrieved from https://www.stats.gov.lc/subjects/society/labour-force/

8. Cunningham, E. (2018, April). Great Recession, great recovery? Trends from the Current Population Survey. *Monthly Labor Review*, U.S. Bureau of Labor Statistics. https://doi.org/10.21916/mlr.2018.10.

9. Government of St. Lucia, Ministry of Finance. (2017). *Percentage contribution of gross domestic product (in constant prices) to the economy, 2007 to 2017*. Economic and Social Review 2017. Retrieved from https://www.stats.gov.lc/subjects/economy/national-accounts/

10. Government of St. Lucia, Central Statistical Office. (2020). *Agriculture, livestock and fishing*. Retrieved from https://www.stats.gov.lc/subjects/economy/agriculture-livestock-and-fishing/

11. International Monetary Fund (IMF). (2002). *St. Lucia: Selected issues and statistical appendix*. Retrieved from https://www.imf.org/external/pubs/ft/scr/2002/cr0214.pdf

12. James, R., Lafeuillee, J., Li, M.X., Salinas,G., and Savchenko, Y. (2019). *Explaining high unemployment in ECCU countries*. International Monetary Fund. Retrieved from http://www.imf.org/en/Publications/WP/

13. Kim, N. (2007). *The impact of remittances on labor supply : the case of Jamaica*. Policy Research Working Paper No. WPS 4120. World Bank. Retrieved from <http://documents.worldbank.org/curated/en/926051468044132562/The-impact-of-remittanceson-labor-supply-the-case-of-Jamaica>

14. World Bank (2005). Organization of Eastern Caribbean States (OECS): *Towards a new agenda for growth*. Retrieved from http://documents.worldbank.org/curated/en/448711468333287677/Organization-of-Eastern-Caribbean-States-OECS-Towards-a-new-agenda-for-growth

15. Government of St. Lucia, Ministry of the Public Service and Human Resource Development. *National ICT strategy of St. Lucia, 2010 - 2015*. Retrieved from http://www.caribbeanelections.com/eDocs/strategy/lc_strategy/lc_National_ICT_Strategy_2010.pdf

16. *St. Lucia News Online*. (2014, November 17). Trade Union Federation accepts three-year public sector wage freeze. Retrieved from https://www.stlucianewsonline.com/trade-union-federation-accepts-three-year-wage-freeze/

17. Prescod, D. (2017, September 30). Our economy — Part 2: Digging a deeper grave. *The Voice*. Retrieved from https://www.thevoiceslu.com/2017/09/economy-part-2-digging-deeper-grave/

18. Macrotrends. (2020). *Barbados Unemployment Rate 1991-2020*. Retrieved from https://www.macrotrends.net/countries/BRB/barbados/unemployment-rate

Chapter 16: The Necessity of Constitutional Change

1. Acemoglu D. and Robinson J.A. (2012). *Why nations fail: The origins of power, prosperity, and poverty*. New York: Currency.

2. Hamer, D. (2004). *Can responsible government survive in Australia?* (pp. 344-354). Canberra, Australia: The Department of the Senate, Parliament House. Retrieved from https://www.aph.gov.au/About_Parliament/Senate/Powers_practice_n_procedures/hamer

3. Schumpeter, J. (1942). *Capitalism, Socialism, and Democracy*. New York: Harper & Bros.

4. Acemoglu D. and Robinson J.A. (2012). *Why nations fail: The origins of power, prosperity, and poverty* (pp. 182-234). New York: Currency.

5. Lansiquot, P. (2020, October 31). Oswald "OzzieBoy" Augustin "shallowness" just can't be helped. *Caribbean News Global*. Retrieved from https://www.caribbeannewsglobal.com/oswald-ozzieboy-augustin-shallowness-just-cant-be-helped/

6. Government of St. Lucia. (2006). *Chapter 1.01: Constitution of Saint Lucia*. Retrieved from http://www.govt.lc/media.govt.lc/www/resources/legislation/ConstitutionOfSaintLucia.pdf

7. Eastern Caribbean Supreme Court. (2020). *Court Overview*. Retrieved from https://www.eccourts.org/court-overview/

8. Caribbean Court of Justice (CCJ). (2020). *About the CCJ*. Retrieved from https://www.ccj.org/about-the-ccj/

9. Government of Saint Lucia. (2011). *Report of the Saint Lucia Constitutional Reform Commission*. Retrieved from http://www.govt.lc/publications/report-of-the-saint-lucia-constitutional-reform-commission

10. Huntley, E.S. (2017, December 9). A deputy essential! So, too, constiutional reform—part 2. *The Voice.* Retrieved from https://www.thevoiceslu.com/2017/12/deputy-essential-constitutional-reform-part-2/

11. Huntley, E.S. (2017, December 2). A deputy essential! So, too, constiutional reform--part 1. *The Voice.* Retrieved from https://www.thevoiceslu.com/2017/12/deputy-essential-constitutional-reform-part-1/

12. UK Parliament (2020). *About Parliament.* Retrieved from https://www.parliament.uk/

13. Larbey, C. (2004, February 11). Will appeal settle Rochamel Case. *The Star,* pp. 1-3.

14. Wayne, R. (2017, April 8). New Law Resurrects Rochamel Controversy! *The Star.* Retrieved from https://stluciastar.com/new-law-resurrects-rochamel-controversy/

15. Micah George, M. (2017, December 30). The Grynberg/St. Lucia matter – an inside look. *The Voice.* Retrieved from https://www.thevoiceslu.com/2017/12/grynberg-st-lucia-matter-inside-look/

16. Giles, C.B. (2011). Democracy at work: A comparative study of the Caribbean State. *The Round Table: The Commonwealth Journal of International Affairs,* 100:414, 285-302. doi: 10.1080/00358533.2011.574902

17. Government of St. Lucia. (2016). *DSH Framework and Supplementary Agreements.* Retrieved from http://www.jakoproductions.com/vieuxfort/DSHAgreements.pdf

18. Jn Baptiste, A. (2020, September 7). The current trajectory of Saint Lucia's development: Part 2. *Caribbean News Global.* Retrieved from https://www.caribbeannewsglobal.com/the-current-trajectory-of-saint-lucias-development-part-2/

19. *Fresh start incentives raise eyebrows.* (2020, July 30). HTS News4orce St. Lucia. Obtained from https://youtu.be/i-KwgFpImuM

20. Untold Stories. (2017, October 28). *The St. Jude reconstruction project documentary part 2.* Retrieved from https://youtu.be/MdRO8q_TyR8

21. George, M. (2017, February 28). $100m. more to complete St. Jude. *The Voice*. Retrieved from https://www.thevoiceslu.com/2017/02/100m-complete-st-jude/

22. Raynold, P. (2005, Spring). The economics of corruption. *The Jako*, pp. 34-42. Retrieved from http://www.jakoproductions.com/culture/TheJakoSpring2005.pdf.

23. King, S. (2020, June 10). Enough is enough. *Caribbean News Global (CNG)*. Retrieved from https://www.caribbeannewsglobal.com/enough-is-enough/

24. HTS St. Lucia (2019, April 5). *Breaking news: minister of government resigns*. Retrieved from HTS4News Force. https://www.htsstlucia.org/breaking-news-minister-of-government-resigns/

INDEX

Philip J. Pierre

Leader of the Opposition St. Lucia Labour Party since 2016.

The World of Anderson Reynolds

"Dr. Reynold's mastery as a fierce storyteller is yet again reaffirmed. This memoir calmly and thoroughly takes the reader along the rough terrain of a family's epic struggle for survival..."
— **Peter Lansiquot, CARICOM economist and diplomat**

"A pulsating ... riveting ... and compellingly readable narrative."
— **Modeste Downes, author of Phases, and Lesson on Wings**

"My Father is No Longer There is a biography and an autobiography, as well as an important addition to our understanding of the unwitting impact of West Indian migration on the psyche of the children involved. It is a love ballad, a joy to read and a privilege to be savoured."
— **Dr. Jolien Harmsen, author of Rum Justice and A History of St. Lucia.**

"The Stall Keeper is an engaging narrative that readers of all ages will find both informative and climactic... An excellent aid to our understanding of our past."
— **The Voice**

"an excellent writer, his characters and situation literally jump off the page,...provides a fascinating and relatable glimpse into a culture that's little known and mysterious to most Americans." — **Writer's Digest**

"The Stall Keeper is arguably the best novel to come out of St. Lucia."
— **Mc Donald Dixon, novelist, poet, and playwright**

"A wonderful journey down memory lane for anyone who has breathed the salty sea breeze of Vieux Fort in the middle and late 20th century... It's a wry book; a story that sticks in the mind."
— **Jolien Harmsen, author of A History of St. Lucia**

"The Struggle for Survival is an important road map of St. Lucia in the pre and post independence period." — **Sir John Compton, Prime Minister of St. Lucia**

"a 206 paged gem ... a powerful commentary ... A deep sincere analytical look into the state of things in the island today. The Struggle For Survival is truly a compendium of St. Lucian life from early times to the modern era ... "
—**Modeste Downes, author of** *Phases*

"... an invaluable book...a source of much information. Much scholarly research has gone into the writing of this work. In a very definite way, establishes the St. Lucian personality, the St. Lucian national and cultural identity."
—**Jacques Compton, Author of** *a troubled dream*

"The Struggle For Survival, although obviously well researched, is an easy-to-read intriguing story of the social and political development of St. Lucia."
—**Travis Weekes, Author of** *Let There Be Jazz*

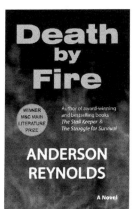

"Death by Fire is an impressive piece of narration ... A veritable tapestry of St. Lucian life and culture ... Easily one of the most compelling pieces of literature I have laid hands on in recent years."
— **Modeste Downes, author of** *Phases*

"The telling of the story is exceptional ... A cunningly-woven tale ... A journey back into St. Lucian life ... (which) paints the dark side of the struggle for survival in a young country."
— **The Voice**

"A novel on a grand scale ... A broad canvas of St. Lucian life ... If one is looking for a key to the feeling and conscience of the age in which we live, this novel is a guide."
—**The Crusader**

Anderson Reynolds was born and raised in Vieux Fort, St. Lucia, where he now resides. He holds a PhD in Food and Resource Economics from the University of Florida. Besides *No Man's Land,* and the memoir, *My Father Is No Longer There,* he is the author of three award-winning and national best-selling books, namely the novels *The Stall Keeper* and *Death by Fire* and the creative *nonfiction The Struggle For Survival: an historical, political, and socioeconomic perspective of St. Lucia.*

Dr. Reynolds' books and newspaper and magazine articles have established him as one of St. Lucia's most prominent and prolific writers and a foremost authority on its socioeconomic history.

Dr. Reynolds' writings, be it fictional or nonfictional, have been described as a world in which a great drama unfolds, where history, geography, nature, culture, the supernatural, and socioeconomic factors all combine to seal the fate of individuals, communities, or for that matter the fate of a whole nation or civilization. In this crucible of a world, readers are provided with deep insights into where St. Lucians come from, who they are as a people, and how they became who they are.

Made in the USA
Columbia, SC
24 November 2024

46929320R00157